ABOUT MATH SUCCESS

W9-CHQ-734

Welcome to Rainbow Bridge Publishing's *Math Success Grade 5*. *Math Success Grade 5* provides students with focused practice to help develop and reinforce math skills in areas appropriate for fifth-grade students. *Math Success Grade 5* uses addition, subtraction, measurement, geometry, fractions, word problems, multiplication, division, and other skills important to mathematical development. In accordance with NCTM (National Council of Teachers of Mathematics) standards, exercises are grade-level appropriate with clear instructions to guide each lesson. Activities help students develop mathematical skills and give students confidence in their ability to work with numbers.

Editor . . . . Carrie Fox
Cover and Layout Design . . . . Chasity Rice
Inside Illustrations. . . . . Chasity Rice
Cover Photo. . . . . Images used under license from Shutterstock, Inc.

65453

ISBN 978-1-60418-046-6

TABLE OF CONTENTS

TABLE OF CONTENTS

Solve each problem.

A.
$$\begin{array}{r} 78 \\ + 11 \\ \hline \end{array}$$
$$\begin{array}{r} 56 \\ - 14 \\ \hline \end{array}$$
$$\begin{array}{r} 483 \\ + 216 \\ \hline \end{array}$$
$$\begin{array}{r} 934 \\ - 114 \\ \hline \end{array}$$
$$\begin{array}{r} 2,384 \\ + 5,612 \\ \hline \end{array}$$

Write the fraction for each shaded part or shade the parts for each fraction given.

B.  ____  ____ $\dfrac{3}{6}$  $\dfrac{2}{5}$

Write each fraction in word form.

C. $\dfrac{3}{8}$ _____ $\dfrac{9}{2}$ _____ $\dfrac{1}{8}$ _____

Solve each problem.

D. $\dfrac{2}{3} + \dfrac{1}{3} =$ $\qquad$ $\dfrac{3}{6} + \dfrac{2}{6} =$ $\qquad$ $\dfrac{8}{9} - \dfrac{2}{9} =$ $\qquad$ $\dfrac{9}{11} - \dfrac{4}{11} =$

Circle the best answer.

E. The length of a desk

   3 in.   3 ft.

   3 yd.   3 mi.

F. The height of a school

   10 cm   10 m

   10 km   10 mm

MATH SUCCESS RB-904107

Solve each problem.

A.
$$64 + 49$$
$$77 - 38$$
$$974 + 238$$
$$686 - 593$$
$$5{,}705 + 5{,}347$$

Write each improper fraction as a mixed number.

B.
$$\frac{15}{2} =$$
$$\frac{45}{4} =$$
$$\frac{33}{8} =$$
$$\frac{29}{3} =$$

Write each mixed number or fraction in simplest form.

C.
$$\frac{15}{30} =$$
$$\frac{18}{27} =$$
$$2\frac{9}{2} =$$
$$5\frac{3}{12} =$$

Solve each problem.

D.
$$\frac{1}{2} \times \frac{3}{4} =$$
$$\frac{5}{9} \times \frac{1}{2} =$$
$$2\frac{1}{3} \times \frac{3}{8} =$$
$$\frac{1}{9} \times 2\frac{1}{12} =$$

Write each fraction as a decimal or decimal as a fraction.

E.
$$5\frac{78}{100} \underline{\hspace{2cm}}$$
$$91\frac{3}{10} \underline{\hspace{2cm}}$$
$$81.2 \underline{\hspace{2cm}}$$
$$0.875 \underline{\hspace{2cm}}$$

Solve each problem.

A.
$$90 \times 7$$

$$772 \times 2$$

$$48 \times 11$$

$$624 \times 18$$

$$8{,}712 \times 36$$

Write each improper fraction as a mixed number. Simplify if possible.

B.
$$\frac{24}{16} =$$

$$\frac{43}{12} =$$

$$\frac{26}{8} =$$

$$\frac{11}{5} =$$

$$\frac{16}{6} =$$

Solve each problem.

C.
$$9 \times \frac{3}{4} =$$

$$\frac{2}{3} \times 4 =$$

$$\frac{1}{6} \times 3\frac{1}{3} =$$

$$\frac{2}{3} \times 5\frac{1}{4} =$$

Convert each measurement.

D.
3 gal. = _____ qt.

12 pt. = _____ cups

5 L = _____ mL

Name the type of figure shown.

E.

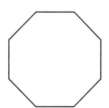 

_____   _____   _____

DIAGNOSTIC TEST 4

Solve each problem.

A. $2\overline{)4}$ $8\overline{)72}$ $5\overline{)115}$ $2\overline{)4,864}$

Rename each fraction using the denominator given.

B. $\dfrac{2}{3} = \dfrac{}{6}$ $\dfrac{4}{5} = \dfrac{}{15}$ $\dfrac{3}{5} = \dfrac{}{20}$ $\dfrac{5}{6} = \dfrac{}{12}$

Find the least common denominator of each fraction pair. Then, rewrite each fraction using the least common denominator.

C. $\dfrac{1}{7} , \dfrac{2}{3}$ $\dfrac{2}{5} , \dfrac{1}{2}$ $\dfrac{3}{4} , \dfrac{1}{5}$

Use >, <, or = to compare each pair of decimals.

D. 6.081 ☐ 6.801   7.006 ☐ 7.06

E. 44.012 ☐ 44.102   212.02 ☐ 212.002

Name the type of angle or line shown.

F.  _____   _____

G. _____   _____

Solve each problem.

A. $15\overline{)46}$ $23\overline{)105}$ $32\overline{)2,528}$ $74\overline{)15,665}$

Solve each problem.

B. $\dfrac{6}{4} + \dfrac{1}{2} =$ $\dfrac{3}{4} - \dfrac{5}{8} =$ $\dfrac{2}{3} + \dfrac{5}{6} =$

Solve each problem.

C. Sam and Mike ordered a large pizza for dinner. There were 12 slices in the pizza. If Sam ate $\dfrac{3}{4}$ of the pizza, how many slices did he eat?

_____

D. Julie had 50 beads. She used 20 beads to make a bracelet. She used 10 beads to make a necklace. What fraction of her beads did Julie have left?

_____

Find the perimeter and area for each figure.

E.
20 cm
8 cm

P = _____

A = _____

F.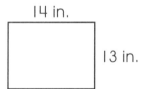
14 in.
13 in.

P = _____

A = _____

MATH SUCCESS RB-904107   © Rainbow Bridge Publishing

DIAGNOSTIC TEST ANALYSIS

After you review students' diagnostic tests, match those problems with incorrect answers to the suggested review pages below. Giving students extra practice and supervision in these trouble areas will help students strengthen their math skills overall.

Diagnostic Test 1
2-, 3-, and 4-Digit Addition and Subtraction
Problem A
Review Pages: 10–23
Identifying and Coloring Fractions
Problems B–C
Review Pages: 51–52, 67–68
Adding and Subtracting Fractions
Problem D
Review Pages: 69–71, 77–78, 88–89
Standard and Metric Length
Problems E–F
Review Pages: 107–108

Diagnostic Test 2
2-, 3-, and 4-Digit Addition and Subtraction
Problem A
Review Pages: 10–22
Writing Improper Fractions as Mixed Numbers
Problem B
Review Pages: 56–57, 67–68
Simplest Form
Problem C
Review Pages: 58–61, 67–68
Multiplying Fractions by Fractions and Mixed Numbers
Problem D
Review Pages: 90–92, 94, 100–101
Equivalent Decimals and Fractions
Problem E
Review Page: 103

Diagnostic Test 3
2-, 3-, and 4-Digit by 1- and 2-Digit Multiplication
Problem A
Review Pages: 24–33
Changing Improper Fractions to Mixed Numbers
Problem B
Review Pages: 54–55, 67–88
Multiplying Fractions by Whole and Mixed Numbers
Problem C
Review Pages: 93–94, 97–100

Standard and Metric Capacity
Problem D
Review Pages: 109–110
Polygons and Geometric Solids
Problem E
Review Pages: 116, 118

Diagnostic Test 4
1-, 2-, 3-, and 4-Digit by 1-Digit Division
Problem A
Review Pages: 34–40, 47–49
Renaming Fractions
Problem B
Review Pages: 62–63, 67–68
Finding the LCD of Fractions
Problem C
Review Pages: 64–65
Comparing Decimals
Problems D–E
Review Pages: 105–106
Lines and Angles
Problems F–G
Review Pages: 114–115

Diagnostic Test 5
2-, 3-, 4-, and 5-Digit by 2-Digit Division
Problem A
Review Pages: 41–50
Adding and Subtracting Fractions with Unlike Denominators
Problem B
Review Pages: 73–74, 76, 81–83, 86–89
Multiplying Fractions Problem Solving
Problem C
Review Pages: 98–101
Fractions Problem Solving
Problem D
Review Pages: 66–68
Perimeter and Area
Problems E–F
Review Pages: 111–113

ADDITION FACTS REVIEW

Solve each problem.

A.	7 + 2	8 + 9	8 + 8	8 + 6	5 + 3	3 + 6	9 + 2
B.	1 + 4	9 + 3	5 + 9	6 + 2	9 + 9	5 + 6	2 + 2
C.	8 + 5	8 + 4	8 + 1	9 + 7	1 + 7	3 + 8	1 + 1
D.	3 + 2	2 + 4	2 + 2	2 + 8	7 + 8	9 + 5	7 + 6
E.	7 + 7	3 + 3	1 + 2	3 + 4	9 + 1	3 + 8	1 + 6
F.	5 + 7	5 + 6	3 + 3	6 + 4	4 + 7	9 + 2	8 + 5
G.	4 + 5	6 + 8	1 + 2	8 + 5	4 + 5	2 + 6	4 + 2
H.	2 + 7	6 + 6	7 + 3	9 + 9	9 + 4	2 + 8	3 + 9
I.	7 + 5	3 + 5	6 + 4	1 + 7	3 + 6	5 + 9	1 + 9
J.	2 + 2	8 + 7	8 + 2	2 + 3	6 + 5	4 + 8	1 + 2

MATH SUCCESS RB-904107

2-DIGIT ADDITION WITHOUT REGROUPING

Add the columns from right to left.   23   Add the **ones**.   23   Add the **tens**.
                                     + 5**4**   + **5**4
                                   _____   _____
                                        7   **7**7

Solve each problem.

A.   20   37   40   40   24   26
   + 11   + 60   + 21   + 13   + 30   + 61

B.   40   13   23   11   66   11
   + 43   + 61   + 36   + 45   + 13   + 80

C.   41   60   23   36   22   10
   + 31   + 35   + 41   + 11   + 67   + 89

D.   50   22   40   83   22   20
   + 36   + 34   + 18   + 16   + 12   + 19

E.   56   22   21   11   24   12
   + 32   + 73   + 58   + 78   + 55   + 40

F.   63   39   13   28   40   59
   + 21   + 30   + 15   + 31   + 36   + 30

G.   63   35   22   35   74   65
   + 14   + 11   + 44   + 31   + 12   + 12

H.   35   23   44   80   61   37
   + 53   + 75   + 34   + 13   + 20   + 50

MATH SUCCESS RB-904107   **11**

3-DIGIT ADDITION WITH AND WITHOUT REGROUPING

Add the columns from right to left.

$\overset{1}{3}\overset{}{4}7$	Add the **ones**.	$\overset{1\,1}{3}47$	Add the **tens**.	$\overset{1\,1}{3}47$	Add the
+ 656	Carry the **ten** to	+ 656	Carry the **hundred** to	+ 656	**hundreds**.
3	the tens column.	03	the hundreds column.	**1,0**03	

Solve each problem. Regroup if needed.

A.
295
+ 610

620
+ 274

681
+ 143

496
+ 674

723
+ 213

B.
829
+ 469

713
+ 847

863
+ 140

648
+ 810

173
+ 726

C.
199
+ 314

480
+ 393

518
+ 622

915
+ 409

249
+ 217

D.
483
+ 195

571
+ 861

266
+ 510

174
+ 717

276
+ 755

E.
163
+ 375

399
+ 196

994
+ 176

946
+ 693

870
+ 519

F.
216
+ 929

805
+ 933

153
+ 386

691
+ 690

119
+ 266

G.
101
+ 928

517
+ 348

601
+ 516

160
+ 993

238
+ 998

MATH SUCCESS RB-904107

4- AND 5-DIGIT ADDITION WITH AND WITHOUT REGROUPING

Add the columns from right to left.

$$
\begin{array}{r} 2,53\mathbf{7} \\ +\ 4,72\mathbf{4} \\ \hline \mathbf{1} \end{array}
\qquad
\begin{array}{r} 2,5\mathbf{3}7 \\ +\ 4,7\mathbf{2}4 \\ \hline \mathbf{6}1 \end{array}
\qquad
\begin{array}{r} 2,\mathbf{5}37 \\ +\ 4,\mathbf{7}24 \\ \hline \mathbf{2}61 \end{array}
\qquad
\begin{array}{r} \mathbf{2},537 \\ +\ \mathbf{4},724 \\ \hline \mathbf{7},261 \end{array}
$$

Solve each problem. Regroup if needed.

A.
$$
\begin{array}{r} 4,510 \\ +\ 4,689 \\ \hline \end{array}
\qquad
\begin{array}{r} 7,166 \\ +\ 5,622 \\ \hline \end{array}
\qquad
\begin{array}{r} 2,198 \\ +\ 2,516 \\ \hline \end{array}
\qquad
\begin{array}{r} 6,043 \\ +\ 6,428 \\ \hline \end{array}
\qquad
\begin{array}{r} 4,025 \\ +\ 1,298 \\ \hline \end{array}
$$

B.
$$
\begin{array}{r} 1,889 \\ +\ 8,458 \\ \hline \end{array}
\qquad
\begin{array}{r} 7,168 \\ +\ 2,362 \\ \hline \end{array}
\qquad
\begin{array}{r} 5,530 \\ +\ 9,022 \\ \hline \end{array}
\qquad
\begin{array}{r} 6,046 \\ +\ 5,539 \\ \hline \end{array}
\qquad
\begin{array}{r} 2,270 \\ +\ 8,696 \\ \hline \end{array}
$$

C.
$$
\begin{array}{r} 8,979 \\ +\ 3,285 \\ \hline \end{array}
\qquad
\begin{array}{r} 5,328 \\ +\ 5,991 \\ \hline \end{array}
\qquad
\begin{array}{r} 6,135 \\ +\ 1,170 \\ \hline \end{array}
\qquad
\begin{array}{r} 2,030 \\ +\ 6,537 \\ \hline \end{array}
\qquad
\begin{array}{r} 1,947 \\ +\ 1,835 \\ \hline \end{array}
$$

D.
$$
\begin{array}{r} 7,564 \\ +\ 5,167 \\ \hline \end{array}
\qquad
\begin{array}{r} 3,504 \\ +\ 1,606 \\ \hline \end{array}
\qquad
\begin{array}{r} 3,044 \\ +\ 4,492 \\ \hline \end{array}
\qquad
\begin{array}{r} 5,013 \\ +\ 8,362 \\ \hline \end{array}
\qquad
\begin{array}{r} 3,501 \\ +\ 4,530 \\ \hline \end{array}
$$

E.
$$
\begin{array}{r} 2,044 \\ +\ 5,367 \\ \hline \end{array}
\qquad
\begin{array}{r} 9,600 \\ +\ 8,664 \\ \hline \end{array}
\qquad
\begin{array}{r} 7,187 \\ +\ 3,436 \\ \hline \end{array}
\qquad
\begin{array}{r} 2,385 \\ +\ 5,652 \\ \hline \end{array}
\qquad
\begin{array}{r} 3,643 \\ +\ 7,244 \\ \hline \end{array}
$$

F.
$$
\begin{array}{r} 28,734 \\ +\ 60,828 \\ \hline \end{array}
\qquad
\begin{array}{r} 55,877 \\ +\ 66,244 \\ \hline \end{array}
\qquad
\begin{array}{r} 46,780 \\ +\ 46,687 \\ \hline \end{array}
\qquad
\begin{array}{r} 65,464 \\ +\ 98,765 \\ \hline \end{array}
\qquad
\begin{array}{r} 24,336 \\ +\ 55,051 \\ \hline \end{array}
$$

G.
$$
\begin{array}{r} 26,634 \\ +\ 24,997 \\ \hline \end{array}
\qquad
\begin{array}{r} 75,019 \\ +\ 82,226 \\ \hline \end{array}
\qquad
\begin{array}{r} 66,777 \\ +\ 16,607 \\ \hline \end{array}
\qquad
\begin{array}{r} 44,041 \\ +\ 17,092 \\ \hline \end{array}
\qquad
\begin{array}{r} 70,292 \\ +\ 40,323 \\ \hline \end{array}
$$

COLUMN ADDITION PRACTICE

Add the columns from right to left.

^{2} 2,75**8**	$^{1\ 2}$ 2,7**58**	$^{2\ 1\ 2}$ 2,**7**58	$^{1\ 2\ 1\ 2}$ **2**,758	$^{1\ 2\ 1\ 2}$ 2,758
17,26**8**	17,2**68**	17,**2**68	1**7**,268	**1**7,268
20,82**0**	20,8**20**	20,**8**20	2**0**,820	**2**0,820
+ 52,31**4**	+ 52,3**14**	+ 52,**3**14	+ 5**2**,314	+ **5**2,314
0	**6**0	**1**60	**3**,160	**9**3,160

Solve each problem.

A.
430	754	174	427	786
978	904	370	140	442
+ 557	+ 723	+ 254	+ 222	+ 209

B.
4,210	9,012	5,816	6,318	2,477
9,733	3,923	1,116	8,833	4,841
+ 1,358	+ 7,725	+ 6,676	+ 7,381	+ 5,713

C.
136	7,164	419	2,342	54,331
435	2,300	6,304	49,534	23,097
257	4,671	2,783	14,735	24,781
+ 375	+ 9,610	+ 8,901	+ 58,561	+ 25,672

D.
253	475	2,742	4,432	4,825
430	234	7,463	9,857	43,029
249	987	4,687	1,248	12,064
475	178	2,115	7,824	16,753
+ 958	+ 572	+ 2,950	+ 5,432	+ 58,439

MATH SUCCESS RB-904107

SUBTRACTION FACTS REVIEW

Solve each problem.

A.	5 − 4	12 − 7	15 − 9	11 − 8	9 − 7	15 − 8	17 − 9	3 − 2
B.	12 − 6	10 − 9	5 − 1	10 − 8	18 − 9	9 − 0	2 − 1	1 − 1
C.	3 − 0	11 − 5	16 − 8	7 − 2	15 − 7	12 − 5	11 − 3	8 − 0
D.	12 − 9	13 − 5	8 − 2	13 − 9	13 − 1	8 − 1	10 − 5	6 − 3
E.	4 − 0	6 − 5	10 − 1	8 − 6	13 − 7	12 − 4	14 − 8	14 − 5
F.	17 − 8	7 − 5	9 − 6	5 − 3	4 − 3	6 − 4	14 − 9	11 − 6
G.	7 − 6	1 − 0	10 − 6	14 − 7	15 − 6	16 − 7	7 − 4	9 − 3
H.	16 − 9	11 − 2	12 − 3	9 − 4	7 − 1	6 − 6	5 − 2	10 − 2
I.	4 − 4	8 − 5	8 − 4	9 − 1	14 − 6	12 − 8	13 − 8	2 − 2
J.	4 − 2	10 − 7	9 − 8	7 − 3	11 − 7	13 − 6	11 − 9	9 − 2

2-DIGIT SUBTRACTION WITHOUT REGROUPING

Subtract the columns from right to left.

```
  27   Subtract the ones.      27   Subtract the tens.      Check:      11
- 16                          - 16                                    + 16
   1                            11                                      27
```

Solve each problem.

A.
```
  79        34        93        47        55        84
- 13      - 20      - 51      - 23      - 21      - 33
```

B.
```
  76        23        70        88        49        37
- 35      - 10      - 30      - 27      - 36      - 21
```

C.
```
  47        76        99        57        45        65
- 17      - 52      - 70      - 17      - 14      - 35
```

D.
```
  29        91        41        59        78        34
- 27      - 81      - 11      - 45      - 27      - 13
```

E.
```
  75        45        72        43        52        64
- 53      - 21      - 21      - 11      - 22      - 22
```

F.
```
  84        47        92        68        74        89
- 12      - 16      - 71      - 33      - 43      - 25
```

G.
```
  97        66        94        27        37        58
- 63      - 12      - 81      - 12      - 16      - 32
```

2-DIGIT SUBTRACTION WITH REGROUPING

Subtract the columns from right to left.

73	Since you cannot subtract 8 from 3,	$\overset{6\ 1}{\cancel{7}3}$ Subtract.	Check:	55
− 18	borrow **ten** from the tens column and add it to the ones column.	− 18		+ 18
		55		73

Solve each problem.

A.
$$\begin{array}{r} 60 \\ -59 \\ \hline \end{array} \qquad \begin{array}{r} 94 \\ -26 \\ \hline \end{array} \qquad \begin{array}{r} 41 \\ -14 \\ \hline \end{array} \qquad \begin{array}{r} 93 \\ -56 \\ \hline \end{array} \qquad \begin{array}{r} 84 \\ -38 \\ \hline \end{array} \qquad \begin{array}{r} 52 \\ -15 \\ \hline \end{array}$$

B.
$$\begin{array}{r} 80 \\ -71 \\ \hline \end{array} \qquad \begin{array}{r} 54 \\ -29 \\ \hline \end{array} \qquad \begin{array}{r} 72 \\ -43 \\ \hline \end{array} \qquad \begin{array}{r} 76 \\ -27 \\ \hline \end{array} \qquad \begin{array}{r} 58 \\ -39 \\ \hline \end{array} \qquad \begin{array}{r} 35 \\ -27 \\ \hline \end{array}$$

C.
$$\begin{array}{r} 80 \\ -75 \\ \hline \end{array} \qquad \begin{array}{r} 31 \\ -25 \\ \hline \end{array} \qquad \begin{array}{r} 91 \\ -18 \\ \hline \end{array} \qquad \begin{array}{r} 51 \\ -25 \\ \hline \end{array} \qquad \begin{array}{r} 67 \\ -28 \\ \hline \end{array} \qquad \begin{array}{r} 43 \\ -39 \\ \hline \end{array}$$

D.
$$\begin{array}{r} 73 \\ -38 \\ \hline \end{array} \qquad \begin{array}{r} 43 \\ -24 \\ \hline \end{array} \qquad \begin{array}{r} 90 \\ -44 \\ \hline \end{array} \qquad \begin{array}{r} 61 \\ -53 \\ \hline \end{array} \qquad \begin{array}{r} 35 \\ -19 \\ \hline \end{array} \qquad \begin{array}{r} 56 \\ -47 \\ \hline \end{array}$$

E.
$$\begin{array}{r} 92 \\ -45 \\ \hline \end{array} \qquad \begin{array}{r} 91 \\ -89 \\ \hline \end{array} \qquad \begin{array}{r} 70 \\ -18 \\ \hline \end{array} \qquad \begin{array}{r} 62 \\ -18 \\ \hline \end{array} \qquad \begin{array}{r} 47 \\ -29 \\ \hline \end{array} \qquad \begin{array}{r} 85 \\ -56 \\ \hline \end{array}$$

F.
$$\begin{array}{r} 62 \\ -26 \\ \hline \end{array} \qquad \begin{array}{r} 91 \\ -82 \\ \hline \end{array} \qquad \begin{array}{r} 61 \\ -53 \\ \hline \end{array} \qquad \begin{array}{r} 82 \\ -73 \\ \hline \end{array} \qquad \begin{array}{r} 74 \\ -59 \\ \hline \end{array} \qquad \begin{array}{r} 32 \\ -26 \\ \hline \end{array}$$

G.
$$\begin{array}{r} 72 \\ -29 \\ \hline \end{array} \qquad \begin{array}{r} 50 \\ -23 \\ \hline \end{array} \qquad \begin{array}{r} 75 \\ -66 \\ \hline \end{array} \qquad \begin{array}{r} 81 \\ -39 \\ \hline \end{array} \qquad \begin{array}{r} 95 \\ -38 \\ \hline \end{array} \qquad \begin{array}{r} 41 \\ -25 \\ \hline \end{array}$$

3-DIGIT SUBTRACTION WITH REGROUPING

Subtract the columns from right to left.

	652	6⁴¹5̸2	Borrow from the tens column. Subtract.	⁵¹⁴¹6̸5̸2	Borrow from the hundreds column. Subtract.	⁵¹⁴¹6̸5̸2	Subtract the hundreds.
	−484	−484		−484		−484	
		8		68		168	

Solve each problem.

A.
$$\begin{array}{r} 738 \\ -264 \end{array}$$
$$\begin{array}{r} 442 \\ -190 \end{array}$$
$$\begin{array}{r} 818 \\ -147 \end{array}$$
$$\begin{array}{r} 965 \\ -466 \end{array}$$
$$\begin{array}{r} 752 \\ -734 \end{array}$$
$$\begin{array}{r} 978 \\ -897 \end{array}$$

B.
$$\begin{array}{r} 993 \\ -295 \end{array}$$
$$\begin{array}{r} 933 \\ -848 \end{array}$$
$$\begin{array}{r} 745 \\ -247 \end{array}$$
$$\begin{array}{r} 953 \\ -539 \end{array}$$
$$\begin{array}{r} 234 \\ -105 \end{array}$$
$$\begin{array}{r} 753 \\ -206 \end{array}$$

C.
$$\begin{array}{r} 893 \\ -647 \end{array}$$
$$\begin{array}{r} 914 \\ -325 \end{array}$$
$$\begin{array}{r} 231 \\ -158 \end{array}$$
$$\begin{array}{r} 752 \\ -743 \end{array}$$
$$\begin{array}{r} 805 \\ -744 \end{array}$$
$$\begin{array}{r} 895 \\ -187 \end{array}$$

D.
$$\begin{array}{r} 632 \\ -247 \end{array}$$
$$\begin{array}{r} 930 \\ -802 \end{array}$$
$$\begin{array}{r} 904 \\ -114 \end{array}$$
$$\begin{array}{r} 618 \\ -229 \end{array}$$
$$\begin{array}{r} 757 \\ -375 \end{array}$$
$$\begin{array}{r} 916 \\ -791 \end{array}$$

E.
$$\begin{array}{r} 745 \\ -673 \end{array}$$
$$\begin{array}{r} 970 \\ -891 \end{array}$$
$$\begin{array}{r} 836 \\ -468 \end{array}$$
$$\begin{array}{r} 152 \\ -144 \end{array}$$
$$\begin{array}{r} 160 \\ -106 \end{array}$$
$$\begin{array}{r} 209 \\ -113 \end{array}$$

F.
$$\begin{array}{r} 819 \\ -141 \end{array}$$
$$\begin{array}{r} 728 \\ -654 \end{array}$$
$$\begin{array}{r} 608 \\ -376 \end{array}$$
$$\begin{array}{r} 928 \\ -581 \end{array}$$
$$\begin{array}{r} 502 \\ -278 \end{array}$$
$$\begin{array}{r} 863 \\ -776 \end{array}$$

G.
$$\begin{array}{r} 481 \\ -328 \end{array}$$
$$\begin{array}{r} 686 \\ -189 \end{array}$$
$$\begin{array}{r} 829 \\ -593 \end{array}$$
$$\begin{array}{r} 558 \\ -268 \end{array}$$
$$\begin{array}{r} 904 \\ -393 \end{array}$$
$$\begin{array}{r} 509 \\ -260 \end{array}$$

MATH SUCCESS RB-904107

4- AND 5-DIGIT SUBTRACTION WITH AND WITHOUT REGROUPING

Subtract the columns from right to left.

$$
\begin{array}{r}
58,235 \\
-\ 7,786 \\
\end{array}
$$

$$
\begin{array}{r}
^{7\ 11\ 12\ 1} \\
5\cancel{8},\cancel{2}\cancel{3}5 \\
-\ 7,786 \\
\hline
\mathbf{50,449} \\
\end{array}
$$

Borrow from the tens column. Continue to borrow as needed to subtract.

Solve each problem. Regroup if needed.

A.
$$\begin{array}{r} 3,186 \\ -\ 2,123 \end{array}$$
$$\begin{array}{r} 7,964 \\ -\ 1,280 \end{array}$$
$$\begin{array}{r} 6,522 \\ -\ 4,910 \end{array}$$
$$\begin{array}{r} 5,885 \\ -\ 5,347 \end{array}$$
$$\begin{array}{r} 6,733 \\ -\ 5,942 \end{array}$$

B.
$$\begin{array}{r} 9,901 \\ -\ 4,576 \end{array}$$
$$\begin{array}{r} 9,483 \\ -\ 7,376 \end{array}$$
$$\begin{array}{r} 8,436 \\ -\ 4,987 \end{array}$$
$$\begin{array}{r} 6,625 \\ -\ 1,784 \end{array}$$
$$\begin{array}{r} 5,167 \\ -\ 1,170 \end{array}$$

C.
$$\begin{array}{r} 85,350 \\ -\ 4,383 \end{array}$$
$$\begin{array}{r} 87,401 \\ -\ 9,289 \end{array}$$
$$\begin{array}{r} 81,761 \\ -\ 1,815 \end{array}$$
$$\begin{array}{r} 97,342 \\ -\ 5,052 \end{array}$$
$$\begin{array}{r} 68,797 \\ -\ 8,749 \end{array}$$

D.
$$\begin{array}{r} 60,721 \\ -\ 9,485 \end{array}$$
$$\begin{array}{r} 66,595 \\ -\ 4,684 \end{array}$$
$$\begin{array}{r} 74,118 \\ -\ 3,982 \end{array}$$
$$\begin{array}{r} 33,688 \\ -\ 1,962 \end{array}$$
$$\begin{array}{r} 97,810 \\ -\ 5,219 \end{array}$$

E.
$$\begin{array}{r} 90,646 \\ -\ 86,247 \end{array}$$
$$\begin{array}{r} 75,460 \\ -\ 16,933 \end{array}$$
$$\begin{array}{r} 46,054 \\ -\ 13,241 \end{array}$$
$$\begin{array}{r} 16,470 \\ -\ 14,549 \end{array}$$
$$\begin{array}{r} 84,192 \\ -\ 39,559 \end{array}$$

F.
$$\begin{array}{r} 99,543 \\ -\ 54,109 \end{array}$$
$$\begin{array}{r} 79,583 \\ -\ 58,149 \end{array}$$
$$\begin{array}{r} 25,911 \\ -\ 20,300 \end{array}$$
$$\begin{array}{r} 51,313 \\ -\ 46,851 \end{array}$$
$$\begin{array}{r} 99,564 \\ -\ 98,300 \end{array}$$

ADDITION AND SUBTRACTION PROBLEM SOLVING

Use the information from the chart to solve each problem.

Football Game Attendance

Game 1	Game 2	Game 3	Game 4	Game 5
1,248	985	879	1,163	2,472

A. How many total seats were filled during the first and second games?

_____

B. How many more people attended the first game than the second?

_____

C. What was the total attendance for all 5 football games?

_____

D. A stadium official estimated that 5,000 people attended the games. How many more people attended the games than was estimated?

_____

E. What was the difference between the most-attended game and the least-attended game?

_____

F. How many total people attended the 3 games with the lowest attendance?

_____

ADDITION AND SUBTRACTION PROBLEM SOLVING

Solve each problem.

A. Mrs. Johnson's fifth-grade class has a goal of reading a total of 2,000 books in four weeks. If the students read 926 books in two weeks, how many more books do they need to read to reach their goal?

_____

B. During the next two weeks, the class read an additional 1,205 books. How many total books have they read? (Hint: Use the information from Question A.)

_____

C. How many more books did they read than their goal of 2,000? (Hint: Use the information from Question B.)

_____

D. Mr. Monson's classroom made a goal to read 3,000 books in four weeks. They read 1,075 books in two weeks. How many more books do they need to read to reach their goal?

_____

E. In the next two weeks, the class read an additional 1,643 books. How many total books did Mr. Monson's class read? (Hint: Use the information from Question D.)

_____

F. Did Mr. Monson's class meet their goal? (Hint: Use the information from Question E.)

_____

Solve each problem.

A.
43	63	308	429	1,249
+ 41	+ 49	+ 769	+ 578	+ 8,764

B.
5,453	83,246	5,449	6,616	24,622
1,628	76,483	3,908	5,431	76,556
+ 8,453	+ 17,758	5,680	4,045	1,154
		+ 5,615	5,483	9,903
			+ 2,944	+ 46,147

C.
24	65	468	578	980
− 12	− 38	− 54	− 38	− 578

D.
859	8,756	5,890	57,897	67,893
− 589	− 4,895	− 3,948	− 5,893	− 57,893

E. Bethany and her mother picked 414 strawberries on Monday, 312 strawberries on Tuesday, and 587 strawberries on Wednesday. How many strawberries did Bethany and her mother pick altogether?

F. Doug sold 447 raffle tickets the first week. He sold 617 raffle tickets the second week. How many more raffle tickets did Doug sell the second week than the first week?

MATH SUCCESS RB-904107

Solve each problem.

A.	35 + 48	47 + 84	348 + 387	273 + 758	5,785 + 2,489

B.	2,478 5,891 + 5,789	84,710 57,892 + 56,982	23 589 901 + 47	457 4,789 9,074 + 5,781	4,893 1,029 47,892 + 57,891

C.	53 − 47	78 − 56	81 − 65	686 − 531	672 − 498

D.	428 − 382	904 − 487	5,783 − 378	7,928 − 5,783	5,789 − 2,891

E.	57,891 − 2,782	89,241 − 4,823	57,891 − 18,472	78,924 − 57,812	90,247 − 78,218

F. Tamika played in a basketball game on Saturday. She scored 22 points in the first two quarters. In the last two quarters, she scored half of the team's 66 points. How many points did Tamika score in the basketball game?

_____

G. Diana decorated 224 cookies on Saturday. On Monday, she decorated another 156 cookies. How many more cookies did Diana decorate on Saturday than on Monday?

_____

MULTIPLICATION FACTS REVIEW

Solve each problem.

A.
$\begin{array}{r} 4 \\ \times\,0 \\ \hline \end{array}$
$\begin{array}{r} 1 \\ \times\,9 \\ \hline \end{array}$
$\begin{array}{r} 5 \\ \times\,9 \\ \hline \end{array}$
$\begin{array}{r} 0 \\ \times\,6 \\ \hline \end{array}$
$\begin{array}{r} 7 \\ \times\,8 \\ \hline \end{array}$
$\begin{array}{r} 6 \\ \times\,4 \\ \hline \end{array}$
$\begin{array}{r} 6 \\ \times\,8 \\ \hline \end{array}$
$\begin{array}{r} 5 \\ \times\,2 \\ \hline \end{array}$

B.
$\begin{array}{r} 2 \\ \times\,6 \\ \hline \end{array}$
$\begin{array}{r} 3 \\ \times\,8 \\ \hline \end{array}$
$\begin{array}{r} 8 \\ \times\,5 \\ \hline \end{array}$
$\begin{array}{r} 7 \\ \times\,5 \\ \hline \end{array}$
$\begin{array}{r} 7 \\ \times\,3 \\ \hline \end{array}$
$\begin{array}{r} 5 \\ \times\,4 \\ \hline \end{array}$
$\begin{array}{r} 3 \\ \times\,6 \\ \hline \end{array}$
$\begin{array}{r} 0 \\ \times\,2 \\ \hline \end{array}$

C.
$\begin{array}{r} 8 \\ \times\,1 \\ \hline \end{array}$
$\begin{array}{r} 1 \\ \times\,7 \\ \hline \end{array}$
$\begin{array}{r} 3 \\ \times\,3 \\ \hline \end{array}$
$\begin{array}{r} 5 \\ \times\,8 \\ \hline \end{array}$
$\begin{array}{r} 6 \\ \times\,7 \\ \hline \end{array}$
$\begin{array}{r} 6 \\ \times\,5 \\ \hline \end{array}$
$\begin{array}{r} 2 \\ \times\,0 \\ \hline \end{array}$
$\begin{array}{r} 4 \\ \times\,8 \\ \hline \end{array}$

D.
$\begin{array}{r} 9 \\ \times\,1 \\ \hline \end{array}$
$\begin{array}{r} 0 \\ \times\,9 \\ \hline \end{array}$
$\begin{array}{r} 9 \\ \times\,6 \\ \hline \end{array}$
$\begin{array}{r} 9 \\ \times\,8 \\ \hline \end{array}$
$\begin{array}{r} 2 \\ \times\,9 \\ \hline \end{array}$
$\begin{array}{r} 7 \\ \times\,7 \\ \hline \end{array}$
$\begin{array}{r} 8 \\ \times\,8 \\ \hline \end{array}$
$\begin{array}{r} 6 \\ \times\,0 \\ \hline \end{array}$

E.
$\begin{array}{r} 9 \\ \times\,5 \\ \hline \end{array}$
$\begin{array}{r} 2 \\ \times\,3 \\ \hline \end{array}$
$\begin{array}{r} 4 \\ \times\,7 \\ \hline \end{array}$
$\begin{array}{r} 9 \\ \times\,8 \\ \hline \end{array}$
$\begin{array}{r} 4 \\ \times\,0 \\ \hline \end{array}$
$\begin{array}{r} 1 \\ \times\,8 \\ \hline \end{array}$
$\begin{array}{r} 8 \\ \times\,3 \\ \hline \end{array}$
$\begin{array}{r} 5 \\ \times\,4 \\ \hline \end{array}$

F.
$\begin{array}{r} 0 \\ \times\,2 \\ \hline \end{array}$
$\begin{array}{r} 6 \\ \times\,2 \\ \hline \end{array}$
$\begin{array}{r} 4 \\ \times\,6 \\ \hline \end{array}$
$\begin{array}{r} 1 \\ \times\,4 \\ \hline \end{array}$
$\begin{array}{r} 3 \\ \times\,5 \\ \hline \end{array}$
$\begin{array}{r} 2 \\ \times\,7 \\ \hline \end{array}$
$\begin{array}{r} 8 \\ \times\,5 \\ \hline \end{array}$
$\begin{array}{r} 5 \\ \times\,3 \\ \hline \end{array}$

G.
$\begin{array}{r} 7 \\ \times\,1 \\ \hline \end{array}$
$\begin{array}{r} 9 \\ \times\,3 \\ \hline \end{array}$
$\begin{array}{r} 3 \\ \times\,7 \\ \hline \end{array}$
$\begin{array}{r} 6 \\ \times\,3 \\ \hline \end{array}$
$\begin{array}{r} 5 \\ \times\,5 \\ \hline \end{array}$
$\begin{array}{r} 7 \\ \times\,4 \\ \hline \end{array}$
$\begin{array}{r} 0 \\ \times\,8 \\ \hline \end{array}$
$\begin{array}{r} 6 \\ \times\,1 \\ \hline \end{array}$

H.
$\begin{array}{r} 7 \\ \times\,6 \\ \hline \end{array}$
$\begin{array}{r} 4 \\ \times\,3 \\ \hline \end{array}$
$\begin{array}{r} 5 \\ \times\,7 \\ \hline \end{array}$
$\begin{array}{r} 2 \\ \times\,8 \\ \hline \end{array}$
$\begin{array}{r} 4 \\ \times\,2 \\ \hline \end{array}$
$\begin{array}{r} 3 \\ \times\,9 \\ \hline \end{array}$
$\begin{array}{r} 0 \\ \times\,3 \\ \hline \end{array}$
$\begin{array}{r} 5 \\ \times\,6 \\ \hline \end{array}$

I.
$\begin{array}{r} 2 \\ \times\,2 \\ \hline \end{array}$
$\begin{array}{r} 6 \\ \times\,4 \\ \hline \end{array}$
$\begin{array}{r} 4 \\ \times\,5 \\ \hline \end{array}$
$\begin{array}{r} 4 \\ \times\,4 \\ \hline \end{array}$
$\begin{array}{r} 3 \\ \times\,1 \\ \hline \end{array}$
$\begin{array}{r} 2 \\ \times\,1 \\ \hline \end{array}$
$\begin{array}{r} 8 \\ \times\,9 \\ \hline \end{array}$
$\begin{array}{r} 5 \\ \times\,1 \\ \hline \end{array}$

J.
$\begin{array}{r} 1 \\ \times\,6 \\ \hline \end{array}$
$\begin{array}{r} 9 \\ \times\,7 \\ \hline \end{array}$
$\begin{array}{r} 9 \\ \times\,9 \\ \hline \end{array}$
$\begin{array}{r} 7 \\ \times\,9 \\ \hline \end{array}$
$\begin{array}{r} 8 \\ \times\,4 \\ \hline \end{array}$
$\begin{array}{r} 0 \\ \times\,6 \\ \hline \end{array}$
$\begin{array}{r} 1 \\ \times\,5 \\ \hline \end{array}$
$\begin{array}{r} 9 \\ \times\,4 \\ \hline \end{array}$

2-DIGIT BY 1-DIGIT MULTIPLICATION

56	56	Multiply the ones.	⁴ 56	Carry the 4 to the tens column.	⁴ 5**6**	Multiply the tens. Add the 4.
× 7	× **7**		× 7		× **7**	
	42		2		392	

Solve each problem.

A.
27	42	49	95	74	78
× 6	× 5	× 7	× 1	× 2	× 8

B.
31	90	34	37	20	18
× 4	× 9	× 2	× 1	× 9	× 7

C.
12	34	37	13	25	73
× 5	× 8	× 9	× 2	× 5	× 7

D.
24	11	64	36	49	43
× 6	× 0	× 5	× 0	× 1	× 4

E.
54	63	62	68	54	70
× 2	× 0	× 3	× 2	× 6	× 3

F.
87	33	61	72	87	10
× 7	× 0	× 8	× 6	× 4	× 1

G.
84	92	45	31	90	69
× 6	× 9	× 5	× 4	× 7	× 2

H.
50	23	41	77	51	88
× 5	× 1	× 2	× 3	× 2	× 0

3-DIGIT BY 1-DIGIT MULTIPLICATION

785 × 3	**1** 7**85** × **3** **5**	Multiply the ones. Put the 5 in the ones place in the answer. Carry the 1 to the tens column.	**2 1** 7**85** × **3** **55**	Multiply the tens. Add the 1. Put the 5 in the tens place in the answer. Carry the 2 to the tens column.

2 1
785
×   **3**
2,355   Multiply 7 × 3. Add the 2.

Solve each problem.

A.
174	649	914	863	717	308
× 2	× 1	× 6	× 5	× 2	× 8

B.
632	998	373	974	875	505
× 4	× 3	× 9	× 3	× 7	× 8

C.
269	499	450	424	279	401
× 6	× 4	× 8	× 5	× 7	× 3

D.
408	859	964	510	772	396
× 6	× 2	× 4	× 9	× 1	× 4

E.
698	774	239	383	353	458
× 7	× 3	× 5	× 2	× 9	× 0

F.
414	279	951	137	708	330
× 4	× 2	× 7	× 9	× 4	× 5

2-DIGIT BY 2-DIGIT MULTIPLICATION

$$
\begin{array}{r} 69 \\ \times\ 35 \end{array}
\qquad
\overset{4}{\underset{345}{\begin{array}{r} 6\mathbf{9} \\ \times\ 3\mathbf{5} \end{array}}} \longleftarrow \mathbf{69} \times \mathbf{5}
\qquad
\text{Multiply by the ones digit.}
$$

Multiply by the ones digit.

$$
\overset{\substack{2\\4}}{\begin{array}{r} 6\mathbf{9} \\ \times\ \mathbf{3}5 \\ \hline 345 \\ 2{,}070 \end{array}} \longleftarrow \mathbf{69} \times \mathbf{30}
$$

Multiply by the tens digit.

$$
\overset{\substack{2\\4}}{\begin{array}{r} 69 \\ \times\ 35 \\ \hline 345 \\ +\ 2{,}070 \\ \hline 2{,}415 \end{array}}
$$

Add the partial products.

Solve each problem.

A.
$\begin{array}{r} 79 \\ \times\ 78 \end{array}$
$\begin{array}{r} 33 \\ \times\ 34 \end{array}$
$\begin{array}{r} 25 \\ \times\ 67 \end{array}$
$\begin{array}{r} 69 \\ \times\ 94 \end{array}$
$\begin{array}{r} 42 \\ \times\ 70 \end{array}$
$\begin{array}{r} 29 \\ \times\ 62 \end{array}$

B.
$\begin{array}{r} 45 \\ \times\ 47 \end{array}$
$\begin{array}{r} 88 \\ \times\ 20 \end{array}$
$\begin{array}{r} 24 \\ \times\ 43 \end{array}$
$\begin{array}{r} 96 \\ \times\ 23 \end{array}$
$\begin{array}{r} 57 \\ \times\ 38 \end{array}$
$\begin{array}{r} 58 \\ \times\ 99 \end{array}$

C.
$\begin{array}{r} 35 \\ \times\ 94 \end{array}$
$\begin{array}{r} 32 \\ \times\ 97 \end{array}$
$\begin{array}{r} 92 \\ \times\ 55 \end{array}$
$\begin{array}{r} 69 \\ \times\ 51 \end{array}$
$\begin{array}{r} 45 \\ \times\ 99 \end{array}$
$\begin{array}{r} 26 \\ \times\ 61 \end{array}$

D.
$\begin{array}{r} 66 \\ \times\ 48 \end{array}$
$\begin{array}{r} 73 \\ \times\ 18 \end{array}$
$\begin{array}{r} 11 \\ \times\ 94 \end{array}$
$\begin{array}{r} 98 \\ \times\ 50 \end{array}$
$\begin{array}{r} 32 \\ \times\ 41 \end{array}$
$\begin{array}{r} 40 \\ \times\ 55 \end{array}$

E.
$\begin{array}{r} 19 \\ \times\ 29 \end{array}$
$\begin{array}{r} 18 \\ \times\ 69 \end{array}$
$\begin{array}{r} 99 \\ \times\ 20 \end{array}$
$\begin{array}{r} 78 \\ \times\ 94 \end{array}$
$\begin{array}{r} 51 \\ \times\ 94 \end{array}$
$\begin{array}{r} 57 \\ \times\ 33 \end{array}$

F.
$\begin{array}{r} 50 \\ \times\ 75 \end{array}$
$\begin{array}{r} 35 \\ \times\ 27 \end{array}$
$\begin{array}{r} 73 \\ \times\ 63 \end{array}$
$\begin{array}{r} 14 \\ \times\ 55 \end{array}$
$\begin{array}{r} 97 \\ \times\ 98 \end{array}$
$\begin{array}{r} 70 \\ \times\ 86 \end{array}$

3-DIGIT BY 2-DIGIT MULTIPLICATION

$$\begin{array}{r} 487 \\ \times\ 29 \end{array}$$

$$\begin{array}{r} ^{7\ 6} \\ \mathbf{487} \\ \times\ 2\mathbf{9} \\ \hline \mathbf{4,383} \end{array} \leftarrow \mathbf{487} \times \mathbf{9}$$

Multiply by the ones digit.

$$\begin{array}{r} ^{|\ |}_{7\ 6} \\ \mathbf{487} \\ \times\ \mathbf{2}9 \\ \hline 4,383 \\ \mathbf{9,740} \end{array} \leftarrow \mathbf{487} \times \mathbf{20}$$

Multiply by the tens digit.

$$\begin{array}{r} ^{|\ |}_{7\ 6} \\ \mathbf{487} \\ \times\ 29 \\ \hline \mathbf{4,383} \\ +\ \mathbf{9,740} \\ \hline \mathbf{14,123} \end{array}$$

Add the partial products.

Solve each problem.

A.
$$\begin{array}{r} 964 \\ \times\ 67 \end{array} \qquad \begin{array}{r} 471 \\ \times\ 23 \end{array} \qquad \begin{array}{r} 268 \\ \times\ 40 \end{array} \qquad \begin{array}{r} 372 \\ \times\ 24 \end{array} \qquad \begin{array}{r} 397 \\ \times\ 46 \end{array} \qquad \begin{array}{r} 140 \\ \times\ 37 \end{array}$$

B.
$$\begin{array}{r} 297 \\ \times\ 80 \end{array} \qquad \begin{array}{r} 117 \\ \times\ 68 \end{array} \qquad \begin{array}{r} 537 \\ \times\ 26 \end{array} \qquad \begin{array}{r} 117 \\ \times\ 79 \end{array} \qquad \begin{array}{r} 976 \\ \times\ 26 \end{array} \qquad \begin{array}{r} 347 \\ \times\ 53 \end{array}$$

C.
$$\begin{array}{r} 447 \\ \times\ 47 \end{array} \qquad \begin{array}{r} 540 \\ \times\ 55 \end{array} \qquad \begin{array}{r} 138 \\ \times\ 95 \end{array} \qquad \begin{array}{r} 294 \\ \times\ 59 \end{array} \qquad \begin{array}{r} 214 \\ \times\ 96 \end{array} \qquad \begin{array}{r} 166 \\ \times\ 39 \end{array}$$

D.
$$\begin{array}{r} 566 \\ \times\ 18 \end{array} \qquad \begin{array}{r} 619 \\ \times\ 84 \end{array} \qquad \begin{array}{r} 125 \\ \times\ 48 \end{array} \qquad \begin{array}{r} 724 \\ \times\ 81 \end{array} \qquad \begin{array}{r} 960 \\ \times\ 69 \end{array} \qquad \begin{array}{r} 435 \\ \times\ 33 \end{array}$$

MATH SUCCESS RB-904107

3- AND 4-DIGIT BY 3-DIGIT MULTIPLICATION

Multiply by the ones digit.	Multiply by the tens digit.	Multiply by the hundreds digit.	Add the partial products.
4 2 1 **8,743** **× 546** **52,458** ↑ **8,743 × 6**	2 1 1 4 2 1 **8,743** **× 546** 52,458 **349,720** ↑ **8,743 × 40**	3 2 1 2 1 1 4 2 1 **8,743** **× 546** 52,458 349,720 **4,371,500** ↑ **8,743 × 500**	3 2 1 2 1 1 4 2 1 8,743 × 546 **52,458** **349,720** **+ 4,371,500** **4,773,678**

Solve each problem.

A.
925	963	916	157	348
× 883	× 500	× 648	× 616	× 216

B.
884	434	754	516	825
× 971	× 251	× 173	× 688	× 409

C.
9,183	7,736	6,949	1,162	3,489
× 217	× 360	× 239	× 957	× 713

MULTIPLICATION PROBLEM SOLVING

Use the information from the chart to solve each problem.

Columbia Elementary students are holding a fund-raiser to buy new computers for their classrooms. They plan on selling dinner tickets to their parents and neighbors and then preparing and serving dinner. Each class has been assigned items to purchase and prepare for the dinner. The local grocery store is advertising the following specials:

Item	Price
Oranges	$1.00 per pound
Cans of Fruit	$2.00 each
Chicken	$5.00 per package
Nuts	$7.00 per pound
Steak	$6.00 per pound

A. Mrs. Browning has volunteered to make a fruit salad for the school fund-raiser. She needs to buy 12 cans of fruit. How much will the 12 cans of fruit cost her?

_____

B. Mrs. Browning also needs to buy oranges. She figures that she will need to purchase 22 pounds of oranges. How much will she have to spend on oranges?

_____

C. Mrs. Browning's recipe calls for two pounds of nuts. She plans on doubling the recipe. How many pounds of nuts will she need?

_____

How much will it cost her?

_____

D. Mr. Willits is in charge of grilling chicken. He figures that he needs to buy 65 packages in order to feed everyone. How much will he have to spend on chicken?

_____

E. Mr. Willits also plans to cook steak for those who do not want to eat chicken. He plans on buying 31 pounds of steak. How much money will he spend on steak?

_____

F. Mr. Willits's class can serve 15 people in one minute. How many people can they serve in 45 minutes?

_____

MATH SUCCESS RB-904107

MULTIPLICATION PROBLEM SOLVING

Use the information to solve each problem.

Mrs. Hamer's class made a goal to complete a total of 1,000 hours of community service during the school year.

A. Randy decided to volunteer at a nursing home. He spent 2 hours per week helping the senior citizens. He volunteered for 23 weeks. How many hours did he volunteer at the nursing home?

_____

B. Ruth spent 5 hours each Saturday for 15 weeks cleaning up the trash on Main Street. How many hours did she volunteer?

_____

C. Thirteen students decided to volunteer at the food bank twice a week for 2 hours each visit. They volunteered for 17 weeks. How many total hours did the 13 students volunteer?

_____

D. Four students worked at the homeless shelter preparing and serving food. They each volunteered for 53 hours. How many hours did the 4 students volunteer altogether?

_____

E. How many total hours did the 19 students in Mrs. Hamer's class (mentioned in the previous problems) volunteer?

_____

Did they meet their goal?

_____

F. If Mr. Jenkins's class of 19 students volunteered together 10 Saturdays in a row for 5 hours each Saturday, how many hours total did they volunteer?

_____

Did Mr. Jenkins's class volunteer more or fewer hours than Mrs. Hamer's class?

_____

Solve each problem.

A.	3 × 7	5 × 6	15 × 9	72 × 8	48 × 3	65 × 7

B.	415 × 5	859 × 6	25 × 57	78 × 19	637 × 8	72 × 8

C.	523 × 38	589 × 57	583 × 902	342 × 421	822 × 45	739 × 502

D.	782 × 718	238 × 890	4,892 × 578	1,328 × 947	2,728 × 454	5,375 × 347

E. Alex can type 43 words per minute. How many words can he type in 11 minutes?

_____

F. Dee's Doughnut Shop makes 36 doughnuts per minute. How many doughnuts can the shop make in 7 minutes?

_____

MATH SUCCESS RB-904107

Solve each problem.

A.
$$5 \times 9$$
$$3 \times 7$$
$$43 \times 8$$
$$76 \times 4$$
$$51 \times 7$$
$$26 \times 3$$

B.
$$234 \times 8$$
$$679 \times 7$$
$$47 \times 46$$
$$48 \times 10$$
$$97 \times 21$$
$$759 \times 6$$

C.
$$534 \times 87$$
$$478 \times 82$$
$$236 \times 743$$
$$924 \times 127$$
$$679 \times 328$$
$$375 \times 371$$

D.
$$593 \times 507$$
$$7,923 \times 783$$
$$4,893 \times 489$$
$$6,781 \times 248$$
$$4,871 \times 628$$
$$2,175 \times 279$$

E. Heidi bought 7 packages of index card labels. Each package contained 48 labels. How many index card labels did she have?

F. Drew labeled 64 test dishes in the science lab. He put 30 seeds in each dish to prepare for an experiment. How many seeds did he use?

DIVISION FACTS REVIEW

Solve each problem.

A. $1\overline{)6}$ $1\overline{)5}$ $8\overline{)48}$ $6\overline{)12}$ $3\overline{)6}$ $1\overline{)4}$ $6\overline{)24}$

B. $2\overline{)4}$ $5\overline{)10}$ $8\overline{)8}$ $7\overline{)56}$ $5\overline{)25}$ $1\overline{)3}$ $2\overline{)18}$

C. $5\overline{)35}$ $7\overline{)14}$ $6\overline{)54}$ $6\overline{)42}$ $4\overline{)12}$ $1\overline{)0}$ $7\overline{)49}$

D. $7\overline{)7}$ $3\overline{)24}$ $4\overline{)36}$ $4\overline{)4}$ $2\overline{)8}$ $9\overline{)54}$ $9\overline{)45}$

E. $6\overline{)48}$ $3\overline{)15}$ $9\overline{)63}$ $8\overline{)64}$ $8\overline{)72}$ $3\overline{)12}$ $1\overline{)1}$

F. $2\overline{)0}$ $2\overline{)6}$ $8\overline{)56}$ $9\overline{)9}$ $2\overline{)14}$ $2\overline{)16}$ $4\overline{)24}$

G. $8\overline{)16}$ $2\overline{)12}$ $2\overline{)4}$ $1\overline{)7}$ $3\overline{)27}$ $3\overline{)6}$ $9\overline{)45}$

H. $9\overline{)81}$ $7\overline{)21}$ $9\overline{)18}$ $7\overline{)42}$ $8\overline{)24}$ $6\overline{)30}$ $7\overline{)63}$

I. $5\overline{)40}$ $2\overline{)10}$ $4\overline{)16}$ $6\overline{)6}$ $3\overline{)3}$ $9\overline{)36}$ $3\overline{)21}$

J. $8\overline{)32}$ $1\overline{)8}$ $5\overline{)45}$ $1\overline{)7}$ $4\overline{)32}$ $9\overline{)72}$ $8\overline{)40}$

1- AND 2-DIGIT BY 1-DIGIT DIVISION

Think:
What number times 3
equals 9?

$3\overline{)9}$

$3 \times \mathbf{3} = 9$

$\mathbf{3}$
$3\overline{)9}$
$\underline{-9}$ Subtract.
0

Solve each problem.

A.　$8\overline{)56}$　　$6\overline{)54}$　　$8\overline{)32}$　　$4\overline{)12}$　　$2\overline{)2}$　　$3\overline{)6}$

B.　$2\overline{)4}$　　$7\overline{)21}$　　$7\overline{)49}$　　$9\overline{)81}$　　$4\overline{)24}$　　$8\overline{)24}$

C.　$5\overline{)45}$　　$5\overline{)30}$　　$7\overline{)28}$　　$9\overline{)72}$　　$3\overline{)3}$　　$6\overline{)30}$

D.　$7\overline{)63}$　　$9\overline{)0}$　　$1\overline{)8}$　　$1\overline{)4}$　　$8\overline{)64}$　　$5\overline{)10}$

E.　$3\overline{)6}$　　$3\overline{)21}$　　$6\overline{)0}$　　$9\overline{)18}$　　$2\overline{)14}$　　$6\overline{)6}$

2-DIGIT BY 1-DIGIT DIVISION

$3\overline{)78}$

Think: What number times 3 is closest to, but less than or equal to, 7?

$3 \times 1 = 3$ too small
$3 \times \mathbf{2} = 6$
$3 \times 3 = 9$ too big

Write 2 over tens column. Write the product of 3×2 under the hundreds column. Subtract and bring down the 8 from the ones column.

$$\begin{array}{r} \mathbf{2} \\ 3\overline{)78} \\ -6\downarrow \\ \hline 18 \end{array}$$

Think: What number times 3 is closest to, but is less than or equal to, 18?

$3 \times \mathbf{6} = 18$

$$\begin{array}{r} 2\mathbf{6} \\ 3\overline{)78} \\ -6 \\ \hline \mathbf{18} \\ -18 \\ \hline 0 \end{array}$$

Solve each problem.

A. $1\overline{)16}$ $8\overline{)96}$ $4\overline{)92}$ $5\overline{)95}$ $3\overline{)99}$

B. $3\overline{)57}$ $1\overline{)11}$ $2\overline{)36}$ $6\overline{)72}$ $6\overline{)84}$

C. $7\overline{)91}$ $9\overline{)72}$ $3\overline{)87}$ $2\overline{)60}$ $4\overline{)84}$

D. $6\overline{)90}$ $9\overline{)54}$ $3\overline{)54}$ $8\overline{)96}$ $5\overline{)85}$

E. $3\overline{)36}$ $6\overline{)24}$ $1\overline{)66}$ $6\overline{)78}$ $6\overline{)66}$

MATH SUCCESS RB-904107   © Rainbow Bridge Publishing

3-DIGIT BY 1-DIGIT DIVISION

$4\overline{)584}$

Think: What number times 4 is closest to, but less than or equal to, 5?
$4 \times 1 = 4$

Subtract and bring down the 8 from the tens column.
Think: What number times 4 is closest to, but less than or equal to, 18? $4 \times 4 = 16$

Subtract and bring down the 4 from the ones column.
Think: What number times 4 is closest to, but less than or equal to, 24? $4 \times 6 = 24$

```
    1
4)584
 - 4
    1
```
Write 1 over the hundreds column. Write the product of 4 x 1 under the hundreds column.

```
   14
4)584
 - 4↓
   18
 - 16
    2
```
Write 4 over the tens column. Write the product of 4 x 4 under the tens and ones columns.

```
   146
4)584
 - 4
   18
 - 16
    24
  -24
     0
```

Solve each problem.

A. $5\overline{)600}$ $2\overline{)320}$ $6\overline{)168}$ $9\overline{)306}$ $3\overline{)846}$

B. $7\overline{)126}$ $5\overline{)190}$ $4\overline{)864}$ $6\overline{)306}$ $8\overline{)128}$

C. $4\overline{)448}$ $5\overline{)135}$ $1\overline{)154}$ $3\overline{)702}$ $2\overline{)204}$

2- AND 3-DIGIT BY 1-DIGIT DIVISION WITH REMAINDERS

$9\overline{)782}$

Think: What number times 9 is closest to, but less than or equal to, 782? (Round to guess.)

$9 \times \mathbf{80} = 720$

Write 8 over the tens column.

$$\begin{array}{r} 8 \\ 9\overline{)782} \\ -72\downarrow \\ \hline 62 \end{array}$$

Think: What number times 9 is closest to, but less than or equal to, 62? (Round to guess.)

$9 \times \mathbf{6} = 54$

$$\begin{array}{r} 8\mathbf{6} \\ 9\overline{)782} \\ -72\downarrow \\ \hline 62 \\ -54 \\ \hline \mathbf{8} \\ \text{remainder} \end{array}$$

$86\ \mathbf{r8}$
$9\overline{)782}$

Solve each problem.

A. $5\overline{)58}$ $6\overline{)79}$ $8\overline{)15}$ $2\overline{)57}$ $3\overline{)80}$

B. $3\overline{)287}$ $9\overline{)498}$ $5\overline{)597}$ $3\overline{)286}$ $2\overline{)483}$

C. $4\overline{)782}$ $6\overline{)351}$ $9\overline{)698}$ $2\overline{)555}$ $4\overline{)489}$

D. $3\overline{)743}$ $7\overline{)219}$ $8\overline{)497}$ $7\overline{)741}$ $6\overline{)784}$

3- AND 4-DIGIT BY 1-DIGIT DIVISION WITH REMAINDERS

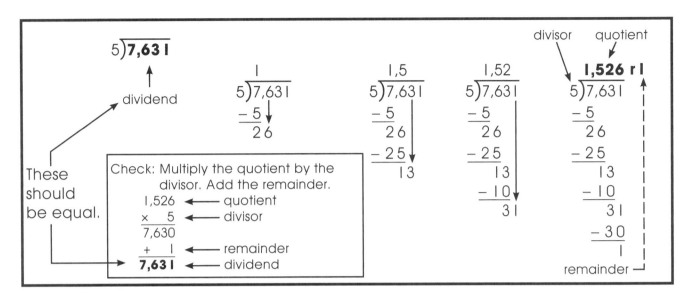

Solve each problem.

A.   7)221   5)101   4)831   2)111   5)583

B.   9)762   2)333   8)890   9)1,382   5)1,587

C.   5)5,844   2)9,285   6)5,818   3)1,118   7)1,324

MATH SUCCESS RB-904107

4-DIGIT BY 1-DIGIT DIVISION WITH REMAINDERS

Think: Can you divide 4 by 6? No. Look at the next number in the dividend. Can you divide 47 by 6? Yes.
6 × **7** = 42

$6\overline{)4,789}$

Write 7 over the hundreds column. Write the product of 6 × 7 under the thousands and hundreds columns.

$$\begin{array}{r} 7 \\ 6\overline{)4,789} \\ -42 \\ \hline 5 \end{array}$$

Subtract and bring down the 8. **Think:** What number times 6 is closest to, but less than or equal to, 58?   6 × **9** = 54

$$\begin{array}{r} 79 \\ 6\overline{)4,789} \\ -42\downarrow \\ \hline 58 \\ -54 \\ \hline 4 \end{array}$$

Write 9 over the tens column. Write the product of 6 × 9 under the hundreds and tens columns.

Subtract and bring down the 9. **Think:** What number times 6 is closest to, but less than or equal to, 49?   6 × **8** = 48

$$\begin{array}{r} 79\mathbf{8}\ \mathbf{r\,1} \\ 6\overline{)4,789} \\ -42 \\ \hline 58 \\ -54\downarrow \\ \hline 49 \\ -48 \\ \hline 1 \end{array}$$

remainder

Solve each problem.

A. $6\overline{)9,773}$ $5\overline{)2,668}$ $8\overline{)6,433}$ $7\overline{)6,301}$ $8\overline{)8,057}$

B. $3\overline{)1,658}$ $4\overline{)6,471}$ $3\overline{)5,720}$ $9\overline{)4,243}$ $3\overline{)1,540}$

C. $9\overline{)5,006}$ $5\overline{)9,378}$ $2\overline{)1,041}$ $7\overline{)4,416}$ $8\overline{)5,745}$

2-DIGIT BY 2-DIGIT DIVISION

$17\overline{)68}$ **Think:** What number times 17 is closest to, but less than or equal to, 68? (Round to guess.)

$$20 \times \textbf{?} = 70$$
$$20 \times \textbf{3} = 60$$
$$17 \times \textbf{3} = 51$$

Try 3:
$$\begin{array}{r} 3 \\ 17\overline{)68} \\ -51 \\ \hline \textbf{17} \end{array}$$

Think: My remainder should always be less than my divisor, so I need to add to my quotient.

Try 4:
$$\begin{array}{r} \textbf{4} \\ 17\overline{)68} \\ -68 \\ \hline 0 \end{array}$$

Solve each problem.

A. $15\overline{)42}$ $23\overline{)47}$ $47\overline{)53}$ $25\overline{)60}$ $36\overline{)52}$

B. $11\overline{)22}$ $12\overline{)20}$ $17\overline{)27}$ $13\overline{)14}$ $20\overline{)20}$

C. $14\overline{)52}$ $12\overline{)48}$ $12\overline{)13}$ $17\overline{)25}$ $38\overline{)84}$

D. $34\overline{)74}$ $19\overline{)26}$ $46\overline{)97}$ $11\overline{)13}$ $26\overline{)88}$

3-DIGIT BY 2-DIGIT DIVISION WITH REMAINDERS

$34\overline{)784}$

Think: What number times 34 is closest to, but less than or equal to, 78? (Round to guess.)

$30 \times ? = 60$
$30 \times 2 = 60$
$34 \times 2 = 68$

Write 2 over the tens column.

$$\begin{array}{r} 2 \\ 34\overline{)784} \\ -68\downarrow \\ \hline 104 \end{array}$$

Think: What number times 34 is closest to, but less than or equal to, 104? (Round to guess.)

$30 \times ? = 100$
$30 \times 3 = 90$
$34 \times 3 = 102$

$$\begin{array}{r} \textbf{23 r2} \\ 34\overline{)784} \\ -68 \\ \hline 104 \\ -102 \\ \hline 2 \end{array}$$

Solve each problem.

A. $88\overline{)784}$ $10\overline{)408}$ $27\overline{)445}$ $61\overline{)274}$ $52\overline{)130}$

B. $13\overline{)708}$ $23\overline{)953}$ $17\overline{)122}$ $87\overline{)687}$ $24\overline{)105}$

C. $23\overline{)101}$ $68\overline{)462}$ $62\overline{)217}$ $46\overline{)391}$ $92\overline{)156}$

MATH SUCCESS RB-904107

3-DIGIT BY 2-DIGIT DIVISION WITH REMAINDERS

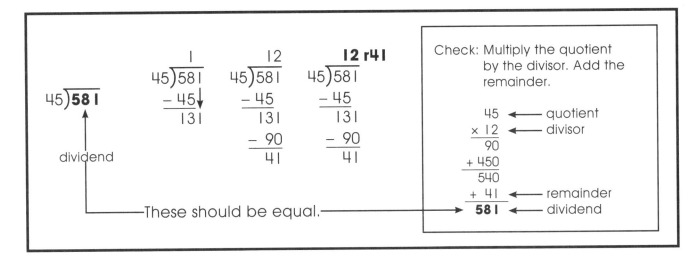

Solve each problem.

A. $46\overline{)441}$ $20\overline{)635}$ $74\overline{)318}$ $22\overline{)415}$ $37\overline{)862}$

B. $81\overline{)569}$ $77\overline{)138}$ $99\overline{)775}$ $56\overline{)875}$ $49\overline{)995}$

C. $18\overline{)296}$ $17\overline{)607}$ $90\overline{)504}$ $62\overline{)586}$ $78\overline{)641}$

4-DIGIT BY 2-DIGIT DIVISION WITH REMAINDERS

$$
\begin{array}{r} 72\overline{)8{,}724} \end{array}
\qquad
\begin{array}{r} 1 \\ 72\overline{)8{,}724} \\ -72\downarrow \\ \hline 152 \end{array}
\qquad
\begin{array}{r} 12 \\ 72\overline{)8{,}724} \\ -72 \\ \hline 152 \\ -144\downarrow \\ \hline 84 \end{array}
\qquad
\begin{array}{r} 121 \\ 72\overline{)8{,}724} \\ -72 \\ \hline 152 \\ -144 \\ \hline 84 \\ -72 \\ \hline 12 \end{array}
\qquad
\begin{array}{r} \mathbf{121\ r12} \\ 72\overline{)8{,}724} \\ -72 \\ \hline 152 \\ -144 \\ \hline 84 \\ -72 \\ \hline 12 \end{array}
$$

Solve each problem.

A. $92\overline{)1{,}274}$ $54\overline{)2{,}809}$ $98\overline{)9{,}108}$ $85\overline{)3{,}950}$

B. $93\overline{)7{,}728}$ $87\overline{)6{,}014}$ $76\overline{)6{,}975}$ $32\overline{)2{,}544}$

C. $74\overline{)4{,}096}$ $13\overline{)3{,}412}$ $30\overline{)2{,}759}$ $42\overline{)6{,}803}$

MATH SUCCESS RB-904107

5-DIGIT BY 2-DIGIT DIVISION WITH REMAINDERS

$$2$$
$$26\overline{)58,631}$$

$$\begin{array}{r}2\\26\overline{)58,631}\\-52\downarrow\\\hline66\end{array}$$

$$\begin{array}{r}22\\26\overline{)58,631}\\-52\\\hline66\\-52\downarrow\\\hline143\end{array}$$

$$\begin{array}{r}225\\26\overline{)58,631}\\-52\\\hline66\\-52\\\hline143\\-130\downarrow\\\hline131\end{array}$$

$$\begin{array}{r}\mathbf{2,255\ r1}\\26\overline{)58,631}\\-52\\\hline66\\-52\\\hline143\\-130\\\hline131\\-130\\\hline1\end{array}$$

Solve each problem.

A. $65\overline{)15,496}$ $32\overline{)23,462}$ $52\overline{)27,966}$ $31\overline{)12,717}$

B. $29\overline{)20,202}$ $72\overline{)42,921}$ $54\overline{)42,780}$ $79\overline{)58,034}$

C. $91\overline{)91,119}$ $53\overline{)51,430}$ $32\overline{)27,215}$ $17\overline{)38,774}$

4- AND 5-DIGIT BY 2-DIGIT DIVISION WITH REMAINDERS

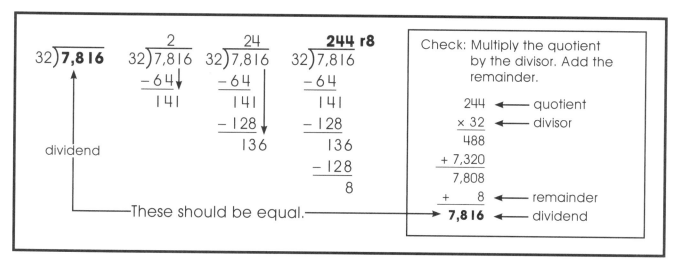

Solve each problem.

A. $43\overline{)9,551}$ $58\overline{)8,150}$ $26\overline{)3,140}$ $15\overline{)1,086}$

B. $34\overline{)9,607}$ $44\overline{)1,125}$ $87\overline{)46,752}$ $42\overline{)29,976}$

C. $45\overline{)24,497}$ $60\overline{)9,607}$ $74\overline{)15,665}$ $85\overline{)3,610}$

MATH SUCCESS RB-904107   © Rainbow Bridge Publishing

DIVISION PROBLEM SOLVING

Solve each problem.

A. Tyree's dad told him that his dog, Sparky, is 91 years old in dog years. If 1 human year is equal to 7 dog years, how many human years has Sparky been alive?

_____

B. Camille states that her dog is only 56 dog years old. If 1 human year is equal to 7 dog years, how many human years has Camille's dog been alive?

_____

C. Katrina found out that 1 human year is about 5 cat years. Her veterinarian told her that her cat was probably about 38 cat years old. How old is Katrina's cat in human years?

_____

What is the remainder?

_____

D. George found out that 1 human year is about 25 rat years. Jason claims that his rat must be 208 in rat years! How many human years old would Jason's rat be in order for his claim to be correct?

_____

What would the remainder be?

_____

E. Latisha asked her teacher, Ms. Sandall, how old she was. Ms. Sandall responded that she is 10,764 days old. Assuming that there are 365 days in a year:

How many years old is Ms. Sandall?

_____

How many days are there until her next birthday?

_____

F. Jerrod has started planning a birthday party for his younger brother Devon. Devon is 851 days old. Assuming that there are 365 days in a year:

How many years old is Devon?

_____

How many days does Jerrod have left to plan Devon's next birthday party?

_____

DIVISION PROBLEM SOLVING

Use the information to solve each problem.

A. Last summer, Martin charged his neighbors $12.00 each time he mowed their lawns. He earned a total of $732.00 over the summer. How many lawns did he mow?

_____

B. This year, Martin decides to begin fertilizing lawns. A 20-pound bag of fertilizer will be enough fertilizer for 5,000 square feet. How many square feet can each pound of fertilizer cover?

_____

C. If Martin plans on mowing 70 lawns next summer, how much should he charge if he wants to earn $910.00?

_____

D. Martin mowed 5 lawns on one Saturday at $12.00 per lawn. At the end of the day, he counted his money. He had $62.00. He remembered that Mrs. Wilson had given him a tip. How much of a tip did she give him?

_____

E. Martin's sister Mindy wants to earn some extra money next summer too. She plans on babysitting. She wants to earn $720.00 over the course of the summer. If Mindy charges $5.00 an hour, how many hours will she have to babysit?

_____

If there are 12 weeks during her summer break, how many hours a week on average will she have to work?

_____

F. During the past three years, Martin has mowed a total of 275 lawns. He charged a different price each year. In all, he earned $4,000.00. How much did Martin charge, on average, to mow a lawn? (Round to the nearest dollar.)

_____

Solve each problem.

A. $3\overline{)72}$ $8\overline{)44}$ $6\overline{)472}$ $3\overline{)852}$

B. $4\overline{)2,408}$ $2\overline{)1,240}$ $16\overline{)67}$ $10\overline{)6,473}$

C. $34\overline{)120}$ $82\overline{)783}$ $92\overline{)3,457}$ $41\overline{)9,056}$

D. $92\overline{)3,457}$ $57\overline{)5,712}$ $21\overline{)39,464}$ $55\overline{)79,432}$

E. Natalie collects glass beads She keeps the beads in small containers that hold 14 beads each. If she has 392 beads, how many containers does she have?

F. Sam and John collected 248 baseball cards. If they put them in groups of 8, how many groups will they have?

Solve each problem.

A. $3\overline{)93}$ $4\overline{)78}$ $6\overline{)375}$ $5\overline{)687}$

B. $3\overline{)4,418}$ $8\overline{)7,243}$ $26\overline{)87}$ $12\overline{)74}$

C. $41\overline{)123}$ $45\overline{)378}$ $82\overline{)7,457}$ $37\overline{)5,775}$

D. $45\overline{)2,875}$ $88\overline{)7,638}$ $89\overline{)19,876}$ $32\overline{)67,814}$

E. Leigh and Denise baked 1,750 brownies for a bake sale. They packed 20 in each box.

How many boxes did they fill?

_____

How many brownies were left?

_____

F. Ray's Lighting Company packs 2,750 lightbulbs into boxes. If each box can hold 35 lightbulbs, how many full boxes are packed?

_____

IDENTIFYING FRACTIONS

A fraction is a part of a whole.

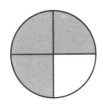 $\frac{3}{4}$ of the circle is shaded. $\frac{1}{4}$ of the circle is not shaded.

$\frac{3}{4}$ ← part shaded   numerator   part not shaded → $\frac{1}{4}$
← total parts   denominator   total parts →

On the first line, write the fraction for the part that is shaded. On the second line, write the fraction for the part that is not shaded.

A.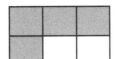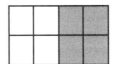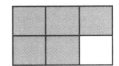

___ ___ ___ ___

B.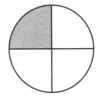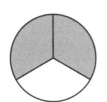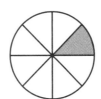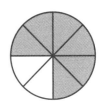

___ ___ ___ ___

C.

___ ___ ___ ___

COLORING FRACTIONS

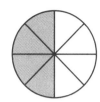 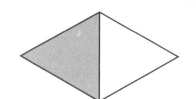

$\frac{4}{8}$ or $\frac{1}{2}$ of the circle is shaded.　　　　$\frac{1}{2}$ of the rhombus is shaded.

Color each shape to show the correct fraction.

A.　$\frac{1}{2}$　　　　　　　$\frac{3}{4}$　　　　　　　$\frac{1}{4}$

B.　$\frac{3}{4}$　　　　　　　$\frac{1}{2}$　　　　　　　$\frac{4}{4}$

C.　$\frac{2}{3}$　　　　　　　$\frac{1}{3}$　　　　　　　$\frac{3}{3}$

D.　$\frac{5}{8}$ 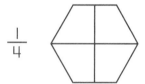　　　$\frac{2}{8}$　　　　　　$\frac{1}{4}$

E.　$\frac{4}{6}$ 　　$\frac{5}{6}$ 　　$\frac{2}{3}$

WRITING FRACTIONS

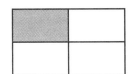

$\frac{1}{4}$ of the rectangle is shaded. $\frac{2}{3}$ of the circle is **not** shaded.

$\frac{1}{4}$ is read as **one-fourth**. $\frac{2}{3}$ is read as **two-thirds**.

Write the following words as fractions.

A. three-fifths _____   three-fourths _____

B. four-ninths _____   one-fourth _____

C. one-third _____   six-twelfths _____

D. two-eighths _____   four-tenths _____

E. four-fifths _____   five-elevenths _____

F. one-half _____   seven-eighths _____

Write each fraction in word form.

G. $\frac{1}{3}$ _____ $\frac{2}{3}$ _____

H. $\frac{1}{2}$ _____ $\frac{1}{8}$ _____

I. $\frac{3}{8}$ _____ $\frac{4}{11}$ _____

J. $\frac{2}{5}$ _____ $\frac{5}{3}$ _____

K. $\frac{5}{7}$ _____ $\frac{5}{9}$ _____

L. $\frac{4}{3}$ _____ $\frac{9}{2}$ _____

WRITING IMPROPER FRACTIONS AS MIXED OR WHOLE NUMBERS

$\frac{14}{3}$ can be rewritten as $14 \div 3$ or $3\overline{)14}$

$\frac{14}{3}$ is an improper fraction.

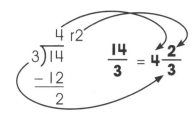

$\frac{14}{3} = 4\frac{2}{3}$

$4\frac{2}{3}$ is a mixed number.

The **4** becomes the whole number. The **2** becomes the numerator of the fraction; the denominator is still **3**.

Write each improper fraction as a mixed or whole number.

A. $\frac{15}{2}$ = $\frac{7}{4}$ = $\frac{20}{7}$ =

B. $\frac{43}{5}$ = $\frac{23}{8}$ = $\frac{21}{5}$ =

C. $\frac{31}{12}$ = $\frac{5}{2}$ = $\frac{13}{8}$ =

D. $\frac{11}{4}$ = $\frac{49}{9}$ = $\frac{41}{6}$ =

E. $\frac{23}{3}$ = $\frac{45}{4}$ = $\frac{60}{5}$ =

F. $\frac{23}{7}$ = $\frac{72}{6}$ = $\frac{16}{2}$ =

WRITING IMPROPER FRACTIONS AS MIXED OR WHOLE NUMBERS

Write each improper fraction as a mixed or whole number.

A. $\dfrac{5}{4}$ = $\dfrac{7}{2}$ = $\dfrac{6}{5}$ =

B. $\dfrac{8}{3}$ = $\dfrac{9}{2}$ = $\dfrac{12}{5}$ =

C. $\dfrac{9}{5}$ = $\dfrac{62}{7}$ = $\dfrac{14}{3}$ =

D. $\dfrac{12}{5}$ = $\dfrac{80}{10}$ = $\dfrac{89}{12}$ =

E. $\dfrac{10}{3}$ = $\dfrac{71}{9}$ = $\dfrac{61}{6}$ =

F. $\dfrac{13}{2}$ = $\dfrac{54}{5}$ = $\dfrac{9}{7}$ =

G. $\dfrac{49}{12}$ = $\dfrac{100}{10}$ = $\dfrac{82}{11}$ =

H. $\dfrac{47}{12}$ = $\dfrac{58}{9}$ = $\dfrac{97}{10}$ =

WRITING MIXED NUMBERS AS IMPROPER FRACTIONS

$$3\frac{1}{3} = \frac{(3 \times 3) + 1}{3}$$
$$= \frac{9 + 1}{3}$$
$$= \frac{10}{3}$$

To change a mixed number to an improper fraction:
1. Multiply the denominator by the whole number.
2. Add the numerator.
3. Keep the denominator.

$$4\frac{5}{8} = \frac{(8 \times 4) + 5}{8}$$
$$= \frac{32 + 5}{8}$$
$$= \frac{37}{8}$$

Write each mixed number as an improper fraction.

A. $2\frac{1}{3} =$ $6\frac{3}{4} =$ $1\frac{1}{12} =$

B. $3\frac{1}{8} =$ $7\frac{3}{5} =$ $1\frac{9}{10} =$

C. $3\frac{2}{5} =$ $9\frac{4}{11} =$ $3\frac{6}{7} =$

D. $5\frac{4}{5} =$ $4\frac{5}{12} =$ $6\frac{7}{11} =$

MATH SUCCESS RB-904107   © Rainbow Bridge Publishing

WRITING MIXED NUMBERS AS IMPROPER FRACTIONS

Write each mixed number as an improper fraction.

A. $3\frac{4}{5} =$ $2\frac{3}{8} =$ $1\frac{5}{12} =$

B. $2\frac{5}{8} =$ $5\frac{3}{4} =$ $8\frac{1}{9} =$

C. $4\frac{2}{3} =$ $6\frac{1}{2} =$ $12\frac{5}{9} =$

D. $7\frac{1}{8} =$ $1\frac{5}{7} =$ $4\frac{8}{11} =$

E. $6\frac{3}{7} =$ $3\frac{2}{5} =$ $7\frac{11}{12} =$

F. $6\frac{7}{8} =$ $2\frac{7}{12} =$ $5\frac{3}{10} =$

MATH SUCCESS RB-904107   **57**

SIMPLIFYING FRACTIONS

$$\frac{4}{8} = \frac{4 \div 4}{8 \div 4}$$

$$= \frac{1}{2}$$

A fraction is simplified when 1 is the only number that divides into both the numerator and the denominator.

To simplify, you must divide the numerator and denominator by the same number.

$$\frac{12}{18} = \frac{12 \div 2}{18 \div 2}$$

$$= \frac{6}{9}$$

$\frac{6}{9}$ is not simplified.

$$\frac{6}{9} = \frac{6 \div 3}{9 \div 3}$$

$$= \frac{2}{3}$$

Write each fraction in simplest form.

A. $\frac{4}{8} =$ $\frac{6}{15} =$ $\frac{8}{24} =$

B. $\frac{4}{6} =$ $\frac{5}{15} =$ $\frac{6}{10} =$

C. $\frac{6}{8} =$ $\frac{2}{24} =$ $\frac{8}{12} =$

D. $\frac{3}{9} =$ $\frac{6}{24} =$ $\frac{10}{12} =$

E. $\frac{6}{12} =$ $\frac{5}{20} =$ $\frac{14}{14} =$

SIMPLIFYING FRACTIONS

Write each fraction in simplest form.

A. $\dfrac{15}{30} =$ $\dfrac{55}{66} =$ $\dfrac{16}{48} =$

B. $\dfrac{10}{24} =$ $\dfrac{6}{72} =$ $\dfrac{24}{36} =$

C. $\dfrac{10}{35} =$ $\dfrac{2}{18} =$ $\dfrac{8}{24} =$

D. $\dfrac{4}{8} =$ $\dfrac{54}{54} =$ $\dfrac{9}{27} =$

E. $\dfrac{7}{21} =$ $\dfrac{15}{25} =$ $\dfrac{25}{50} =$

F. $\dfrac{6}{18} =$ $\dfrac{9}{12} =$ $\dfrac{2}{16} =$

G. $\dfrac{18}{27} =$ $\dfrac{14}{40} =$ $\dfrac{9}{18} =$

H. $\dfrac{6}{15} =$ $\dfrac{12}{36} =$ $\dfrac{6}{9} =$

SIMPLIFYING MIXED NUMBERS

$2\dfrac{5}{15} = 2 + \dfrac{5}{15}$

$\quad = 2 + \dfrac{5 \div 5}{15 \div 5}$

$\quad = 2 + \dfrac{1}{3}$

$\quad = \mathbf{2\dfrac{1}{3}}$

When simplifying mixed numbers, simplify the fractions.

$3\dfrac{9}{6} = 3 + \dfrac{9}{6}$

$\quad = 3 + \dfrac{9 \div 3}{6 \div 3}$

$\quad = 3 + \dfrac{3}{2}$

Change to a mixed number.

$\quad = 3 + 1\dfrac{1}{2}$

$\quad = 3 + 1 + \dfrac{1}{2} = \mathbf{4\dfrac{1}{2}}$

Write each mixed number in simplest form.

A. $2\dfrac{2}{4} =$ $3\dfrac{5}{15} =$ $2\dfrac{12}{16} =$

B. $1\dfrac{6}{9} =$ $2\dfrac{9}{2} =$ $6\dfrac{3}{3} =$

C. $2\dfrac{5}{20} =$ $4\dfrac{7}{21} =$ $5\dfrac{9}{6} =$

D. $4\dfrac{9}{3} =$ $5\dfrac{3}{12} =$ $2\dfrac{3}{2} =$

SIMPLEST FORM

Write each fraction in simplest form.

A. $\frac{6}{18}$ = $\frac{12}{18}$ = $\frac{20}{24}$ =

B. $\frac{18}{24}$ = $\frac{9}{54}$ = $\frac{6}{12}$ =

Write each fraction as a mixed number. Simplify if possible.

C. $\frac{9}{8}$ = $\frac{11}{5}$ = $\frac{16}{6}$ =

D. $\frac{16}{3}$ = $\frac{24}{16}$ = $\frac{18}{4}$ =

Write each mixed number in simplest form.

E. $1\frac{5}{15}$ = $2\frac{4}{6}$ = $4\frac{3}{12}$ =

F. $5\frac{8}{6}$ = $4\frac{18}{24}$ = $3\frac{9}{2}$ =

RENAMING FRACTIONS

To rename a fraction, multiply the numerator and denominator by the same number.

$$\frac{1}{3} = \frac{1 \times 2}{3 \times 2} = \frac{2}{6}$$

$\frac{1}{3}$ of the circle is shaded.

$\frac{2}{6}$ of the circle is shaded.

$$\frac{4}{5} \longrightarrow \overline{10}$$

Think: To get from 5 to 10, multiply by 2.

So, $\frac{4}{5} = \frac{4 \times 2}{5 \times 2} = \frac{8}{10}$

$$\frac{2}{3} \longrightarrow \overline{12}$$

Think: To get from 3 to 12, multiply by 4.

So, $\frac{2}{3} = \frac{2 \times 4}{3 \times 4} = \frac{8}{12}$

Rename each fraction using the denominator given.

A. $\frac{3}{4} = \frac{}{12}$ $\frac{4}{5} = \frac{}{15}$ $\frac{2}{3} = \frac{}{6}$

B. $\frac{1}{4} = \frac{}{16}$ $\frac{5}{6} = \frac{}{18}$ $\frac{3}{5} = \frac{}{20}$

C. $\frac{5}{8} = \frac{}{24}$ $\frac{2}{7} = \frac{}{14}$ $\frac{5}{6} = \frac{}{12}$

MATH SUCCESS RB-904107

RENAMING FRACTIONS

$$\frac{2}{5} \longrightarrow \overline{15} \qquad\qquad 4 = \frac{}{2} \quad \textbf{Think: } 4 = \frac{4}{1}$$

$$\frac{4}{1} \longrightarrow \frac{}{2}$$

$$\text{So, } \frac{2}{5} = \frac{2 \times 3}{5 \times 3} = \frac{\textbf{6}}{\textbf{15}} \qquad\qquad \text{So, } \frac{4}{1} = \frac{4 \times 2}{1 \times 2} = \frac{\textbf{8}}{\textbf{2}}$$

Rename each fraction using the denominator given.

A. $\frac{1}{2} = \frac{}{8}$ $\qquad\qquad \frac{2}{3} = \frac{}{30}$ $\qquad\qquad \frac{3}{4} = \frac{}{20}$

B. $\frac{3}{5} = \frac{}{15}$ $\qquad\qquad \frac{1}{5} = \frac{}{50}$ $\qquad\qquad \frac{11}{12} = \frac{}{48}$

C. $\frac{1}{4} = \frac{}{12}$ $\qquad\qquad \frac{4}{9} = \frac{}{81}$ $\qquad\qquad \frac{5}{9} = \frac{}{18}$

D. $\frac{1}{3} = \frac{}{15}$ $\qquad\qquad \frac{2}{7} = \frac{}{21}$ $\qquad\qquad \frac{3}{4} = \frac{}{16}$

FINDING THE LCD OF FRACTIONS

The least common denominator (LCD) for two fractions is the least common multiple of the denominators.

To find the LCD:
1. List the multiples of each denominator.
2. The LCD is the least common multiple.

Example: Find the LCD of $\frac{2}{3}$ and $\frac{3}{4}$. Rewrite each fraction using the LCD.

1. List the multiples of each denominator.

3 = 3, 6, 9, (12) 15, 18, 21, 24, . . .
4 = 4, 8, (12) 16, 20, 24, . . .

2. The LCD = 12.

$\frac{2}{3} = \frac{}{12}$ ⟵———— LCD of 3 and 4

$\frac{2}{3} = \frac{2 \times 4}{3 \times 4} = \frac{8}{12}$

$\frac{2}{3} = \frac{8}{12}$

$\frac{3}{4} = \frac{}{12}$ ⟵———— LCD of 3 and 4

$\frac{3}{4} = \frac{3 \times 3}{4 \times 3} = \frac{9}{12}$

$\frac{3}{4} = \frac{9}{12}$

Find the LCD of each pair of fractions. Then, rewrite each fraction using the new common denominator.

A. $\frac{2}{3}$, $\frac{4}{5}$ $\frac{1}{2}$, $\frac{1}{3}$ $\frac{2}{5}$, $\frac{1}{2}$

B. $\frac{3}{4}$, $\frac{1}{5}$ $\frac{1}{7}$, $\frac{2}{3}$ $\frac{6}{7}$, $\frac{1}{3}$

C. $\frac{1}{2}$, $\frac{3}{5}$ $\frac{4}{7}$, $\frac{1}{2}$ $\frac{2}{3}$, $\frac{5}{8}$

USING THE LCD TO ADD AND SUBTRACT FRACTIONS

To add and subtract fractions, they must have the same denominator. If they do not have the same denominator, find the least common denominator by listing the multiples of each denominator. Rewrite each fraction using the LCD. Then, add or subtract.

$$\frac{3}{6} + \frac{4}{10}$$

1. List the multiples of each denominator.
   6 = 6, 12, 18, 24, ㉚ . . .
   10 = 10, 20, ㉚ . . .
   The LCD is 30.

2. $\frac{3}{6} = \frac{15}{30}$; $\frac{4}{10} = \frac{12}{30}$

   $\frac{15}{30} + \frac{12}{30} = \frac{27}{30}$

Find the LCD of each pair of fractions. Then, rewrite each fraction using the new common denominator and add or subtract the fractions.

A. $\frac{2}{3} + \frac{5}{6}$ $\qquad\qquad$ $\frac{1}{2} - \frac{1}{4}$ $\qquad\qquad$ $\frac{2}{5} + \frac{1}{10}$

B. $\frac{3}{4} + \frac{1}{12}$ $\qquad\qquad$ $\frac{1}{7} - \frac{2}{14}$ $\qquad\qquad$ $\frac{6}{9} - \frac{1}{3}$

C. $\frac{1}{10} + \frac{3}{5}$ $\qquad\qquad$ $\frac{3}{8} + \frac{1}{2}$ $\qquad\qquad$ $\frac{3}{4} - \frac{5}{8}$

FRACTIONS PROBLEM SOLVING

Use the information to solve each problem.

> **Math Treats**
>
> $2\frac{1}{2}$ cups peanut butter
>
> $1\frac{2}{8}$ cups honey
>
> $2\frac{1}{2}$ teaspoons vanilla
>
> $5\frac{5}{2}$ cups coconut
>
> $\frac{5}{2}$ cups raisins

You want to make math treats, but you have only 4 measuring items—1 cup, $\frac{1}{4}$ cup, $\frac{1}{3}$ cup, and $\frac{1}{2}$ teaspoon.

A. You measure 2 cups of peanut butter into the mixing bowl. How many $\frac{1}{4}$ cups will you need to complete the recipe?

_____

B. Will you use your $\frac{1}{4}$ cup or $\frac{1}{3}$ cup to measure the honey?

_____

C. Write the improper fraction for the amount of vanilla you will need to add.

_____

D. How many cups of coconut will you need to add? (Do not include an improper fraction.)

_____

E. How many cups of raisins will you need? (Do not include an improper fraction.)

_____

F. What ingredient do you add the most of?

_____

MATH SUCCESS RB-904107

Write the fraction for the part that is shaded.

A.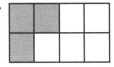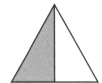

_____   _____   _____   _____

Write each improper fraction as a mixed number.

B. $\dfrac{8}{3} =$ $\dfrac{7}{5} =$ $\dfrac{9}{2} =$

Write each mixed number as an improper fraction.

C. $2\dfrac{3}{4} =$ $4\dfrac{3}{7} =$ $5\dfrac{1}{2} =$

Write each fraction in simplest form.

D. $\dfrac{4}{6} =$ $\dfrac{5}{15} =$ $\dfrac{4}{18} =$

Rename each fraction using the denominator given.

E. $\dfrac{3}{4} = \dfrac{}{16}$ $\dfrac{2}{3} = \dfrac{}{21}$ $\dfrac{1}{6} = \dfrac{}{18}$

Solve each problem.

F. Julie and Sarah ordered a large pizza for dinner. There were 16 slices in the pizza. If Julie ate $\dfrac{2}{8}$ of the pizza, how many slices did she eat?

G. Jen had 60 stickers. She gave 10 stickers to her friend, 15 stickers to her sister, and 20 stickers to her cousin. What fraction of her stickers does Jen have left?

_____   _____

Write each improper fraction as a mixed number.

A. $\dfrac{7}{3} =$ $\dfrac{11}{5} =$ $\dfrac{5}{2} =$ $\dfrac{9}{8} =$

Write each mixed number as an improper fraction.

B. $1\dfrac{3}{5} =$ $4\dfrac{2}{3} =$ $5\dfrac{1}{6} =$ $3\dfrac{5}{8} =$

Write each fraction in simplest form.

C. $\dfrac{15}{20} =$ $\dfrac{4}{12} =$ $\dfrac{2}{16} =$ $\dfrac{6}{20} =$

Rename each fraction using the denominator given.

D. $\dfrac{1}{4} = \dfrac{}{12}$ $\dfrac{4}{6} = \dfrac{}{24}$ $\dfrac{4}{5} = \dfrac{}{25}$ $\dfrac{2}{9} = \dfrac{}{27}$

Solve each problem.

E. Grant had 60 minutes to take his history test. He spent 10 minutes on the true/false questions, 15 minutes on the short answer questions, and 20 minutes on the essay. What fraction of the time was left to check his work?

F. Antonio had 85 baseball cards. He sold 40 cards to his friend José. What fraction of his baseball cards did Antonio keep?

ADDING FRACTIONS

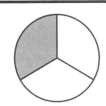 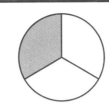 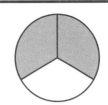

$$\frac{1}{3} \quad + \quad \frac{1}{3} \quad = \quad \frac{2}{3}$$

Use the information given to fill in each blank and/or shade each unshaded object.

A.

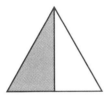 + 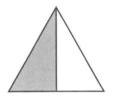 =

_____ + _____ = _____

B.

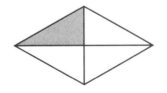 + 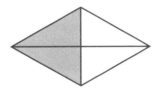 =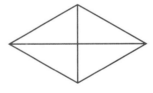

_____ + _____ = _____

C.

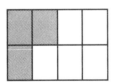 + 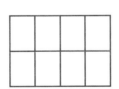 =

_____ + $\frac{2}{8}$ = _____

D.

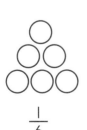 + =

$\frac{1}{6}$ + _____ = _____

ADDING FRACTIONS

When adding fractions with like denominators:

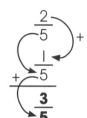

1. Add the numerators.
2. Keep the same denominator.
3. Simplify if possible.

$$\frac{5}{12} + \frac{5}{12} = \frac{10}{12} = \frac{5}{6}$$

Solve each problem. Simplify if possible.

A.
$$\frac{3}{5} + \frac{1}{5}$$
$$\frac{1}{3} + \frac{1}{3}$$
$$\frac{1}{6} + \frac{3}{6}$$
$$\frac{1}{9} + \frac{2}{9}$$

B.
$$\frac{1}{7} + \frac{2}{7}$$
$$\frac{1}{4} + \frac{1}{4}$$
$$\frac{1}{12} + \frac{4}{12}$$
$$\frac{3}{10} + \frac{4}{10}$$

C.
$$\frac{3}{6} + \frac{2}{6}$$
$$\frac{1}{11} + \frac{3}{11}$$
$$\frac{3}{8} + \frac{3}{8}$$
$$\frac{4}{9} + \frac{3}{9}$$

D.
$$\frac{2}{9} + \frac{2}{9}$$
$$\frac{3}{12} + \frac{5}{12}$$
$$\frac{5}{11} + \frac{2}{11}$$
$$\frac{5}{8} + \frac{2}{8}$$

ADDING FRACTIONS

$$\begin{array}{r} \dfrac{3}{7} \\[2mm] + \dfrac{6}{7} \\ \hline \dfrac{9}{7} \end{array} = 1\dfrac{2}{7}$$

Add.

Simplify.

$$\begin{array}{r} \dfrac{7}{8} \\[2mm] + \dfrac{5}{8} \\ \hline \dfrac{12}{8} \end{array} = 1\dfrac{4}{8} = 1\dfrac{1}{2}$$

Solve each problem. Simplify if possible.

A.
$$\begin{array}{r} \dfrac{2}{6} \\ + \dfrac{4}{6} \\ \hline \end{array}$$
$$\begin{array}{r} \dfrac{2}{3} \\ + \dfrac{2}{3} \\ \hline \end{array}$$
$$\begin{array}{r} \dfrac{6}{7} \\ + \dfrac{2}{7} \\ \hline \end{array}$$
$$\begin{array}{r} \dfrac{3}{10} \\ + \dfrac{2}{10} \\ \hline \end{array}$$

B.
$$\begin{array}{r} \dfrac{2}{5} \\ + \dfrac{4}{5} \\ \hline \end{array}$$
$$\begin{array}{r} \dfrac{5}{12} \\ + \dfrac{1}{12} \\ \hline \end{array}$$
$$\begin{array}{r} \dfrac{1}{2} \\ + \dfrac{1}{2} \\ \hline \end{array}$$
$$\begin{array}{r} \dfrac{4}{6} \\ + \dfrac{5}{6} \\ \hline \end{array}$$

C.
$$\begin{array}{r} \dfrac{4}{7} \\ + \dfrac{5}{7} \\ \hline \end{array}$$
$$\begin{array}{r} \dfrac{3}{8} \\ + \dfrac{2}{8} \\ \hline \end{array}$$
$$\begin{array}{r} \dfrac{5}{6} \\ + \dfrac{5}{6} \\ \hline \end{array}$$
$$\begin{array}{r} \dfrac{2}{9} \\ + \dfrac{4}{9} \\ \hline \end{array}$$

D.
$$\begin{array}{r} \dfrac{7}{10} \\ + \dfrac{5}{10} \\ \hline \end{array}$$
$$\begin{array}{r} \dfrac{3}{4} \\ + \dfrac{3}{4} \\ \hline \end{array}$$
$$\begin{array}{r} \dfrac{7}{8} \\ + \dfrac{3}{8} \\ \hline \end{array}$$
$$\begin{array}{r} \dfrac{7}{12} \\ + \dfrac{9}{12} \\ \hline \end{array}$$

ADDING MIXED NUMBERS

When adding mixed numbers:

$3\frac{2}{6}$

$+\ 2\frac{1}{6}$

$5\frac{3}{6} = \mathbf{5\frac{1}{2}}$

1. Add the fractions.
2. Add the whole numbers.
3. Simplify if possible.

$2\frac{5}{12}$

$+\ 1\frac{11}{12}$

$3\frac{16}{12} = 3 + 1 + \frac{4}{12} = \mathbf{4\frac{1}{3}}$

Solve each problem. Simplify if possible.

A.

$3\frac{1}{3}$ $\qquad$ $4\frac{2}{5}$ $\qquad$ $3\frac{3}{8}$ $\qquad$ $7\frac{3}{4}$

$+\ 2\frac{1}{3}$ $\qquad$ $+\ \ \frac{1}{5}$ $\qquad$ $+\ 2\frac{5}{8}$ $\qquad$ $+\ 5\frac{3}{4}$

B.

$2\frac{4}{5}$ $\qquad$ $13\frac{5}{8}$ $\qquad$ $1\frac{3}{4}$ $\qquad$ $4\frac{1}{7}$

$+\ 3\frac{2}{5}$ $\qquad$ $+\ \ \frac{7}{8}$ $\qquad$ $+\ 2\frac{3}{4}$ $\qquad$ $+\ 2\frac{2}{7}$

C.

$10\frac{2}{9}$ $\qquad$ $3\frac{5}{6}$ $\qquad$ $2\frac{7}{10}$ $\qquad$ $3\frac{3}{5}$

$+\ 2\frac{7}{9}$ $\qquad$ $+\ 2\frac{3}{6}$ $\qquad$ $+\ 1\frac{4}{10}$ $\qquad$ $+\ 1\frac{1}{5}$

D.

$5\frac{4}{8}$ $\qquad$ $3\frac{7}{12}$ $\qquad$ $8\frac{7}{9}$ $\qquad$ $23\frac{4}{10}$

$+\ \ \frac{2}{8}$ $\qquad$ $+\ 4\frac{9}{12}$ $\qquad$ $+\ 9\frac{5}{9}$ $\qquad$ $+\ 17\frac{7}{10}$

ADDING FRACTIONS WITH UNLIKE DENOMINATORS

When adding fractions with unlike denominators:

$$\frac{2}{3} \longrightarrow \frac{2 \times 4}{3 \times 4} \longrightarrow \frac{8}{12}$$

$$+\frac{1}{4} \longrightarrow \frac{1 \times 3}{4 \times 3} \longrightarrow \frac{3}{12}$$

$$\frac{11}{12}$$

1. Find the least common denominator (LCD).
2. Rewrite each fraction using the LCD.
3. Add.
4. Simplify if possible.

$$\frac{5}{6} \longrightarrow \frac{5 \times 5}{6 \times 5} \longrightarrow \frac{25}{30}$$

$$+\frac{2}{5} \longrightarrow \frac{2 \times 6}{5 \times 6} \longrightarrow \frac{12}{30}$$

$$\frac{37}{30}$$

$$= 1\frac{7}{30}$$

Solve each problem. Simplify if possible.

A.
$$\frac{2}{5}$$
$$+\frac{1}{3}$$

$$\frac{3}{8}$$
$$+\frac{1}{3}$$

$$\frac{1}{2}$$
$$+\frac{1}{3}$$

$$\frac{3}{4}$$
$$+\frac{3}{5}$$

B.
$$\frac{5}{6}$$
$$+\frac{2}{5}$$

$$\frac{2}{7}$$
$$+\frac{2}{3}$$

$$\frac{3}{10}$$
$$+\frac{1}{3}$$

$$\frac{5}{9}$$
$$+\frac{1}{2}$$

C.
$$\frac{3}{4}$$
$$+\frac{1}{7}$$

$$\frac{1}{3}$$
$$+\frac{5}{8}$$

$$\frac{1}{3}$$
$$+\frac{3}{4}$$

$$\frac{7}{10}$$
$$+\frac{2}{3}$$

ADDING FRACTIONS WITH UNLIKE DENOMINATORS

When adding fractions with unlike denominators:

$$\frac{1}{6} \longrightarrow \frac{1}{6}$$

$$\frac{2}{+\ 3} \longrightarrow \frac{2\times 2}{3\times 2} \longrightarrow \frac{4}{6}$$

$$\frac{5}{6}$$

1. Find the least common denominator (LCD).
2. Rewrite each fraction using the LCD.
3. Add.
4. Simplify if possible.

$$\frac{5}{6} \longrightarrow \frac{5\times 2}{6\times 2} \longrightarrow \frac{10}{12}$$

$$\frac{7}{+\ 12} \longrightarrow \frac{7}{12}$$

$$\frac{17}{12}$$

$$= 1\frac{5}{12}$$

Solve each problem. Simplify if possible.

A.

$$\frac{2}{3}$$
$$+\ \frac{4}{9}$$

$$\frac{1}{4}$$
$$+\ \frac{5}{8}$$

$$\frac{3}{5}$$
$$+\ \frac{1}{10}$$

$$\frac{5}{8}$$
$$+\ \frac{1}{2}$$

B.

$$\frac{1}{3}$$
$$+\ \frac{5}{6}$$

$$\frac{1}{5}$$
$$+\ \frac{4}{15}$$

$$\frac{1}{6}$$
$$+\ \frac{2}{3}$$

$$\frac{7}{8}$$
$$+\ \frac{3}{4}$$

C.

$$\frac{1}{2}$$
$$+\ \frac{7}{8}$$

$$\frac{5}{8}$$
$$+\ \frac{1}{4}$$

$$\frac{6}{7}$$
$$+\ \frac{1}{14}$$

$$\frac{5}{12}$$
$$+\ \frac{5}{6}$$

ADDING MIXED NUMBERS WITH UNLIKE DENOMINATORS

When adding fractions with unlike denominators:

$$2\frac{1}{3} \longrightarrow \frac{1 \times 4}{3 \times 4} \longrightarrow \frac{4}{12}$$

$$+3\frac{3}{4} \longrightarrow \frac{3 \times 3}{4 \times 3} \longrightarrow \frac{9}{12}$$

$$5 \qquad\qquad\qquad \frac{13}{12}$$

$$= 5 + 1\frac{1}{12} = \mathbf{6\frac{1}{12}}$$

1. Find the least common denominator (LCD).
2. Rewrite each fraction using the LCD.
3. Add.
4. Simplify if possible.

$$1\frac{7}{8} \longrightarrow \frac{7}{8}$$

$$+2\frac{1}{4} \longrightarrow \frac{1 \times 2}{4 \times 2} \longrightarrow \frac{2}{8}$$

$$3 \qquad\qquad\qquad \frac{9}{8}$$

$$= 3 + 1\frac{1}{8} = \mathbf{4\frac{1}{8}}$$

Solve each problem. Simplify if possible.

A.
$$1\frac{3}{8}$$ $$+4\frac{1}{6}$$

$$2\frac{3}{4}$$ $$+3\frac{1}{5}$$

$$5\frac{1}{3}$$ $$+1\frac{5}{6}$$

$$3\frac{2}{3}$$ $$+2\frac{1}{4}$$

B.
$$6\frac{1}{2}$$ $$+1\frac{3}{4}$$

$$5\frac{2}{5}$$ $$+2\frac{1}{3}$$

$$4\frac{1}{6}$$ $$+2\frac{3}{4}$$

$$1\frac{7}{8}$$ $$+2\frac{1}{6}$$

C.
$$4\frac{5}{12}$$ $$+2\frac{5}{6}$$

$$1\frac{2}{5}$$ $$+3\frac{7}{10}$$

$$2\frac{3}{8}$$ $$+7\frac{1}{2}$$

$$6\frac{7}{11}$$ $$+5\frac{1}{2}$$

ADDING FRACTIONS AND MIXED NUMBERS

Solve each problem. Simplify if possible.

A.
$$\frac{1}{8} + \frac{3}{8}$$
$$\frac{5}{12} + \frac{1}{12}$$
$$\frac{1}{5} + \frac{1}{5}$$
$$\frac{8}{9} + \frac{4}{9}$$

B.
$$2\frac{1}{3} + \frac{1}{3}$$
$$3\frac{1}{4} + 5\frac{3}{4}$$
$$\frac{5}{6} + 2\frac{1}{6}$$
$$4\frac{2}{9} + 5\frac{1}{9}$$

C.
$$3\frac{1}{4} + \frac{2}{7}$$
$$5\frac{3}{5} + \frac{1}{7}$$
$$5\frac{3}{11} + \frac{9}{11}$$
$$\frac{5}{6} + \frac{1}{3}$$

D.
$$\frac{5}{8} + \frac{5}{6}$$
$$\frac{3}{4} + \frac{1}{5}$$
$$\frac{1}{5} + \frac{6}{15}$$
$$\frac{1}{8} + \frac{5}{12}$$

E.
$$5\frac{5}{6} + 2\frac{1}{3}$$
$$5\frac{1}{3} + 2\frac{1}{8}$$
$$4\frac{1}{9} + 2\frac{1}{6}$$
$$1\frac{1}{5} + 3\frac{3}{10}$$

MATH SUCCESS RB-904107

SUBTRACTING FRACTIONS

When subtracting fractions with like denominators:

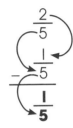

$\dfrac{2}{5}$

$-\dfrac{1}{5}$

$\dfrac{1}{5}$

1. Subtract the numerators.
2. Keep the same denominator.
3. Simplify if possible.

$\dfrac{7}{8}$

$-\dfrac{3}{8}$

$\dfrac{4}{8} = \dfrac{1}{2}$

Solve each problem. Simplify if possible.

A.

$\dfrac{3}{8}$
$-\dfrac{1}{8}$

$\dfrac{7}{12}$
$-\dfrac{5}{12}$

$\dfrac{5}{6}$
$-\dfrac{1}{6}$

$\dfrac{6}{7}$
$-\dfrac{3}{7}$

B.

$\dfrac{11}{12}$
$-\dfrac{1}{12}$

$\dfrac{9}{10}$
$-\dfrac{3}{10}$

$\dfrac{4}{5}$
$-\dfrac{2}{5}$

$\dfrac{2}{3}$
$-\dfrac{1}{3}$

C.

$\dfrac{3}{4}$
$-\dfrac{1}{4}$

$\dfrac{11}{12}$
$-\dfrac{5}{12}$

$\dfrac{10}{11}$
$-\dfrac{3}{11}$

$\dfrac{13}{16}$
$-\dfrac{3}{16}$

SUBTRACTING FRACTIONS FROM WHOLE NUMBERS

When subtracting a fraction from a whole number:

$$3 \longrightarrow 2\frac{4}{4}$$
$$-\frac{1}{4} \longrightarrow \frac{1}{4}$$
$$2\frac{3}{4}$$

1. Rewrite the whole number as an equivalent fraction using the LCD.
2. Subtract.

$$2 \longrightarrow 1\frac{6}{6}$$
$$-\frac{5}{6} \longrightarrow \frac{5}{6}$$
$$1\frac{1}{6}$$

Solve each problem.

A.
$$5 \quad\quad 3 \quad\quad 6 \quad\quad 4$$
$$-\frac{7}{8} \quad\quad -\frac{1}{3} \quad\quad -\frac{7}{9} \quad\quad -\frac{2}{5}$$

B.
$$8 \quad\quad 5 \quad\quad 12 \quad\quad 9$$
$$-\frac{4}{5} \quad\quad -\frac{4}{9} \quad\quad -\frac{3}{11} \quad\quad -\frac{8}{9}$$

C.
$$7 \quad\quad 10 \quad\quad 12 \quad\quad 8$$
$$-\frac{1}{3} \quad\quad -\frac{1}{5} \quad\quad -\frac{7}{10} \quad\quad -\frac{5}{6}$$

MATH SUCCESS RB-904107

SUBTRACTING MIXED NUMBERS

Rewrite $3\frac{1}{4}$ so that you can subtract.

$$3\frac{1}{4} = 2 + 1\frac{1}{4} = 2\frac{5}{4}$$

$$-1\frac{3}{4} \longrightarrow 1\frac{3}{4}$$

$$1\frac{2}{4} = 1\frac{1}{2}$$

Rewrite $6\frac{2}{9}$ so that you can subtract.

$$6\frac{2}{9} = 5 + 1\frac{2}{9} = 5\frac{11}{9}$$

$$-5\frac{4}{9} \longrightarrow 5\frac{4}{9}$$

$$\frac{7}{9}$$

Solve each problem. Simplify if possible.

A.
$$3\frac{3}{7} \\ -1\frac{5}{7}$$

$$5\frac{1}{3} \\ -2\frac{2}{3}$$

$$4\frac{1}{6} \\ -3\frac{5}{6}$$

$$8\frac{3}{8} \\ -2\frac{5}{8}$$

B.
$$6\frac{1}{5} \\ -3\frac{3}{5}$$

$$4\frac{3}{10} \\ -3\frac{7}{10}$$

$$8\frac{2}{5} \\ -5\frac{4}{5}$$

$$10\frac{5}{12} \\ -7\frac{7}{12}$$

C.
$$3\frac{1}{8} \\ -2\frac{5}{8}$$

$$6\frac{4}{9} \\ -5\frac{7}{9}$$

$$12\frac{5}{12} \\ -10\frac{7}{12}$$

$$9\frac{1}{4} \\ -3\frac{3}{4}$$

SUBTRACTING MIXED NUMBERS

Solve each problem. Simplify if possible.

A.
$$5\frac{1}{4}$$
$$-\ 2\frac{3}{4}$$

$$7\frac{3}{7}$$
$$-\ 5\frac{4}{7}$$

$$8\frac{5}{12}$$
$$-\ 7\frac{11}{12}$$

$$4\frac{3}{8}$$
$$-\ 2\frac{5}{8}$$

B.
$$5\frac{1}{4}$$
$$-\ 2\frac{3}{4}$$

$$7\frac{3}{7}$$
$$-\ 5\frac{4}{7}$$

$$5\frac{1}{8}$$
$$-\ 2\frac{7}{8}$$

$$8\frac{3}{10}$$
$$-\ 3\frac{7}{10}$$

C.
$$10\frac{1}{7}$$
$$-\ 9\frac{6}{7}$$

$$8\frac{3}{10}$$
$$-\ 5\frac{7}{10}$$

$$5\frac{2}{5}$$
$$-\ 1\frac{4}{5}$$

$$6\frac{1}{6}$$
$$-\ 2\frac{5}{6}$$

D.
$$2\frac{6}{11}$$
$$-\ 1\frac{8}{11}$$

$$5\frac{1}{3}$$
$$-\ 4\frac{2}{3}$$

$$7\frac{1}{5}$$
$$-\ 4\frac{2}{5}$$

$$10\frac{2}{10}$$
$$-\ 9\frac{7}{10}$$

E.
$$6\frac{2}{6}$$
$$-\ 1\frac{5}{6}$$

$$8\frac{3}{7}$$
$$-\ 2\frac{5}{7}$$

$$7\frac{1}{4}$$
$$-\ 2\frac{3}{4}$$

$$12\frac{1}{3}$$
$$-\ 2\frac{2}{3}$$

MATH SUCCESS RB-904107

SUBTRACTING FRACTIONS WITH UNLIKE DENOMINATORS

When subtracting fractions with unlike denominators:

$$\frac{2}{5} \rightarrow \frac{2 \times 3}{5 \times 3} \rightarrow \frac{6}{15}$$

$$-\frac{1}{3} \rightarrow \frac{1 \times 5}{3 \times 5} \rightarrow \frac{5}{15}$$

$$\frac{1}{15}$$

1. Find the least common denominator.
2. Rewrite fractions using the LCD.
3. Subtract.

$$\frac{5}{8} \rightarrow \frac{5 \times 3}{8 \times 3} \rightarrow \frac{15}{24}$$

$$-\frac{1}{3} \rightarrow \frac{1 \times 8}{3 \times 8} \rightarrow \frac{8}{24}$$

$$\frac{7}{24}$$

Solve each problem. Simplify if possible.

A.
$$\frac{2}{3}$$
$$-\frac{1}{4}$$

$$\frac{4}{5}$$
$$-\frac{1}{2}$$

$$\frac{1}{2}$$
$$-\frac{1}{3}$$

$$\frac{5}{7}$$
$$-\frac{1}{2}$$

B.
$$\frac{1}{2}$$
$$-\frac{2}{9}$$

$$\frac{2}{3}$$
$$-\frac{2}{7}$$

$$\frac{3}{4}$$
$$-\frac{1}{5}$$

$$\frac{4}{5}$$
$$-\frac{2}{7}$$

C.
$$\frac{3}{5}$$
$$-\frac{2}{9}$$

$$\frac{7}{8}$$
$$-\frac{2}{5}$$

$$\frac{5}{6}$$
$$-\frac{1}{7}$$

$$\frac{9}{11}$$
$$-\frac{1}{6}$$

SUBTRACTING FRACTIONS WITH UNLIKE DENOMINATORS

When subtracting fractions with unlike denominators:

$$\frac{3}{4} \rightarrow \frac{3 \times 3}{4 \times 3} \rightarrow \frac{9}{12}$$

$$\frac{1}{-6} \rightarrow \frac{1 \times 2}{6 \times 2} \rightarrow \frac{2}{12}$$

$$\frac{\mathbf{7}}{\mathbf{12}}$$

1. Find the least common denominator.
2. Rewrite fractions using the LCD.
3. Subtract.
4. Simplify if possible.

$$\frac{7}{12} \longrightarrow \frac{7}{12}$$

$$\frac{1}{-4} \rightarrow \frac{1 \times 3}{4 \times 3} \rightarrow \frac{3}{12}$$

$$\frac{4}{12} = \frac{\mathbf{1}}{\mathbf{3}}$$

Solve each problem. Simplify if possible.

A.
$$\frac{3}{4} \quad \frac{7}{9} \quad \frac{1}{2} \quad \frac{2}{3}$$
$$-\frac{7}{10} \quad -\frac{1}{6} \quad -\frac{3}{8} \quad -\frac{2}{9}$$

B.
$$\frac{7}{12} \quad \frac{7}{10} \quad \frac{3}{4} \quad \frac{3}{10}$$
$$-\frac{1}{4} \quad -\frac{1}{2} \quad -\frac{3}{8} \quad -\frac{1}{5}$$

C.
$$\frac{5}{8} \quad \frac{5}{6} \quad \frac{3}{4} \quad \frac{7}{8}$$
$$-\frac{1}{6} \quad -\frac{3}{10} \quad -\frac{1}{6} \quad -\frac{5}{6}$$

 MATH SUCCESS RB-904107

SUBTRACTING FRACTIONS WITH UNLIKE DENOMINATORS

Solve each problem. Simplify if possible.

A.
$$\frac{1}{2} - \frac{1}{3}$$
$$\frac{4}{5} - \frac{1}{6}$$
$$\frac{3}{4} - \frac{1}{6}$$
$$\frac{3}{5} - \frac{1}{2}$$

B.
$$\frac{3}{4} - \frac{3}{8}$$
$$\frac{1}{2} - \frac{3}{10}$$
$$\frac{1}{2} - \frac{1}{4}$$
$$\frac{7}{8} - \frac{1}{2}$$

C.
$$\frac{5}{8} - \frac{1}{3}$$
$$\frac{4}{5} - \frac{3}{10}$$
$$\frac{2}{3} - \frac{2}{9}$$
$$\frac{5}{6} - \frac{4}{9}$$

D.
$$\frac{5}{8} - \frac{1}{6}$$
$$\frac{11}{12} - \frac{3}{4}$$
$$\frac{2}{3} - \frac{1}{4}$$
$$\frac{5}{6} - \frac{1}{2}$$

E.
$$\frac{2}{3} - \frac{1}{6}$$
$$\frac{3}{4} - \frac{2}{5}$$
$$\frac{5}{12} - \frac{1}{3}$$
$$\frac{4}{5} - \frac{2}{3}$$

MATH SUCCESS RB-904107

SUBTRACTING MIXED NUMBERS

Steps 1 & 2 **Step 3**

$8\dfrac{1}{3} \rightarrow 8\dfrac{8}{24} \rightarrow 7\dfrac{32}{24}$

$-\,6\dfrac{5}{8} \rightarrow 6\dfrac{15}{24} \rightarrow 6\dfrac{15}{24}$

$1\dfrac{17}{24}$

Step 3

$8\dfrac{8}{24} = 7 + 1 + \dfrac{8}{24}$

$= 7 + \dfrac{24}{24} + \dfrac{8}{24}$

$= 7 + \dfrac{\mathbf{32}}{\mathbf{24}}$

When subtracting mixed numbers:

1. Find the least common denominator.
2. Rewrite fractions using the LCD.
3. Rewrite again, if needed, to subtract.
4. Subtract.
5. Simplify if possible.

Solve each problem. Simplify if possible.

A.

$4\dfrac{1}{3}$ $\qquad$ $6\dfrac{1}{8}$ $\qquad$ $5\dfrac{1}{4}$ $\qquad$ $8\dfrac{3}{5}$

$-\,2\dfrac{1}{2}$ $\qquad$ $-\,5\dfrac{1}{6}$ $\qquad$ $-\,3\dfrac{1}{2}$ $\qquad$ $-\,5\dfrac{1}{3}$

B.

$6\dfrac{3}{8}$ $\qquad$ $4\dfrac{2}{9}$ $\qquad$ $9\dfrac{1}{6}$ $\qquad$ $5\dfrac{2}{5}$

$-\,5\dfrac{3}{4}$ $\qquad$ $-\,3\dfrac{2}{3}$ $\qquad$ $-\,7\dfrac{1}{3}$ $\qquad$ $-\,3\dfrac{7}{10}$

C.

$6\dfrac{1}{3}$ $\qquad$ $7\dfrac{1}{4}$ $\qquad$ $9\dfrac{3}{10}$ $\qquad$ $3\dfrac{5}{12}$

$-\,4\dfrac{5}{8}$ $\qquad$ $-\,3\dfrac{7}{8}$ $\qquad$ $-\,5\dfrac{4}{5}$ $\qquad$ $-\,2\dfrac{2}{3}$

SUBTRACTING FRACTIONS AND MIXED NUMBERS

Solve each problem. Simplify if possible.

A.
$$\frac{3}{4} - \frac{1}{4}$$
$$\frac{6}{7} - \frac{2}{3}$$
$$5\frac{1}{3} - 2\frac{2}{3}$$
$$6 - \frac{7}{8}$$

B.
$$\frac{4}{5} - \frac{1}{2}$$
$$\frac{3}{8} - \frac{1}{4}$$
$$2\frac{5}{6} - \frac{1}{3}$$
$$7\frac{7}{8} - \frac{3}{8}$$

C.
$$\frac{5}{12} - \frac{1}{12}$$
$$8\frac{7}{8} - 2\frac{3}{8}$$
$$9\frac{3}{4} - 3\frac{1}{3}$$
$$2\frac{1}{3} - \frac{4}{5}$$

D.
$$11\frac{3}{5} - 2\frac{1}{5}$$
$$4\frac{4}{5} - \frac{8}{10}$$
$$\frac{7}{11} - \frac{1}{3}$$
$$\frac{5}{8} - \frac{4}{12}$$

E.
$$9\frac{2}{3} - \frac{2}{3}$$
$$\frac{7}{12} - \frac{5}{12}$$
$$2 - \frac{5}{6}$$
$$10\frac{3}{8} - 9\frac{3}{4}$$

ADDING AND SUBTRACTING FRACTIONS PROBLEM SOLVING

Use the information to solve each problem.

Rachel, Grant, Ethan, and Sarah are competing in an obstacle course. The course is 1 mile long. Each person must complete one part of the competition. The course includes running through tires for $\frac{1}{6}$ mile, dribbling a basketball for $\frac{1}{4}$ mile, running for $\frac{1}{2}$ mile, and crossing a row of monkey bars.

A. If Rachel runs through the tires for $\frac{1}{6}$ of a mile and Grant dribbles the basketball for $\frac{1}{4}$ mile, what fraction of the course have Rachel and Grant completed?

_____

B. If Ethan then runs for $\frac{1}{2}$ mile, how much of the course have Rachel, Grant, and Ethan completed?

_____

What fraction of the 1-mile course must Sarah cross on the monkey bars?

_____

C. What fraction of the course did the boys cover?

_____

What fraction did the girls cover?

_____

D. It took the team 25 minutes to complete the race. If it took Rachel $5\frac{1}{3}$ minutes, Grant $7\frac{1}{4}$ minutes, and Sarah $6\frac{1}{6}$ minutes, how long did it take Ethan to run the $\frac{1}{2}$ mile?

_____

ADDING AND SUBTRACTING FRACTIONS PROBLEM SOLVING

Use the information to solve each problem.

Jobs	Tanya's Time per Job	Tyrell's Time per Job
Homework	$2\frac{1}{4}$ hours	$1\frac{2}{3}$ hours
Clean Bathroom	$\frac{3}{4}$ hour	$\frac{1}{2}$ hour
Clean Bedroom	$\frac{1}{3}$ hour	1 hour
Walk Dog	$\frac{1}{2}$ hour	$\frac{3}{4}$ hour

A. How much total time does it take both Tanya and Tyrell to do their homework?

_____

B. How much more time does Tanya spend on her homework than Tyrell spends on his?

_____

C. How much more time does Tyrell spend cleaning his bedroom than Tanya spends cleaning hers?

_____

D. If Tyrell comes home from school, does his homework, and then walks the dog, how much time will it take him?

_____

E. If Tanya cleans only once a week, how much time does she spend cleaning the bathroom and bedroom per week?

_____

F. If Tyrell cleans the bathroom twice a week and Tanya cleans the bathroom only once a week, who spends more time cleaning the bathroom?

_____

Solve each problem. Simplify if possible.

A.
$$\frac{3}{5}$$
$$+\ \frac{1}{5}$$

$$\frac{5}{12}$$
$$+\ \frac{1}{12}$$

$$\frac{4}{5}$$
$$+\ \frac{4}{5}$$

$$\frac{1}{6}$$
$$+\ \frac{5}{6}$$

B.
$$2\frac{3}{8}$$
$$+\ 1\frac{1}{8}$$

$$5\frac{1}{3}$$
$$+\ \frac{1}{3}$$

$$7\frac{4}{7}$$
$$+\ 8\frac{5}{7}$$

$$9\frac{5}{12}$$
$$+\ 3\frac{7}{12}$$

C.
$$\frac{7}{8}$$
$$-\ \frac{1}{8}$$

$$2\frac{4}{5}$$
$$-\ 1\frac{1}{5}$$

$$3\frac{1}{4}$$
$$-\ 2\frac{3}{4}$$

$$5\frac{9}{12}$$
$$-\ 3\frac{11}{12}$$

D.
$$\frac{11}{12}$$
$$-\ \frac{5}{6}$$

$$\frac{5}{8}$$
$$-\ \frac{1}{6}$$

$$7\frac{5}{7}$$
$$-\ 2\frac{3}{7}$$

$$13\frac{2}{5}$$
$$-\ 8\frac{8}{15}$$

E. Sam ate $\frac{2}{3}$ of a pizza. Joe ate $\frac{1}{9}$ of the same pizza. How much of the pizza is left?

F. Jane has a bag of beads. She used $\frac{9}{16}$ of the beads to make a necklace. She glued $\frac{2}{8}$ of the beads on a picture frame. What fraction of the beads did Jane use?

MATH SUCCESS RB-904107

Solve each problem. Simplify if possible.

A. $\dfrac{3}{7}$ $+\dfrac{1}{7}$ $\dfrac{7}{12}$ $+\dfrac{5}{12}$ $\dfrac{4}{9}$ $+\dfrac{2}{9}$ $\dfrac{5}{6}$ $+\dfrac{5}{6}$

B. $2\dfrac{3}{10}$ $+1\dfrac{1}{10}$ $8\dfrac{1}{3}$ $+\dfrac{2}{3}$ $2\dfrac{3}{8}$ $+8\dfrac{5}{8}$ $1\dfrac{5}{12}$ $+3\dfrac{1}{12}$

C. $\dfrac{5}{8}$ $-\dfrac{1}{8}$ $4\dfrac{4}{5}$ $-1\dfrac{2}{5}$ $5\dfrac{1}{4}$ $-3\dfrac{3}{4}$ $7\dfrac{3}{12}$ $-3\dfrac{7}{12}$

D. $\dfrac{2}{3}$ $-\dfrac{1}{6}$ $\dfrac{11}{12}$ $-\dfrac{5}{6}$ 7 $-\dfrac{3}{7}$ $21\dfrac{2}{15}$ $-8\dfrac{4}{5}$

E. Mr. Thomas's class raised $\dfrac{3}{8}$ of the money for a class party. If Juan's mom gave the class $\dfrac{10}{16}$ of the money they needed, can they have their party?

_____

F. The mail carrier delivered $\dfrac{3}{10}$ of the mail in her bag in the morning. If she delivered $\dfrac{1}{5}$ of the mail in the afternoon, how much of the mail is left in her bag?

_____

MULTIPLYING FRACTIONS

$\frac{1}{2} \times \frac{1}{4}$ can be visualized as:

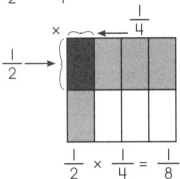

$$\frac{1}{2} \times \frac{1}{4} = \frac{1}{8}$$

$\frac{2}{3} \times \frac{4}{5}$ can be visualized as:

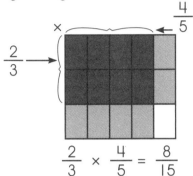

$$\frac{2}{3} \times \frac{4}{5} = \frac{8}{15}$$

Use the grids to solve each problem.

A.

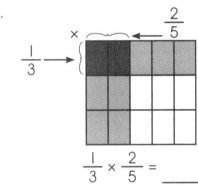

$$\frac{1}{3} \times \frac{2}{5} = \underline{\hspace{1cm}}$$

B.

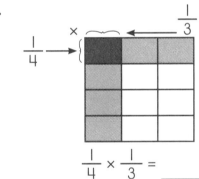

$$\frac{1}{4} \times \frac{1}{3} = \underline{\hspace{1cm}}$$

C.

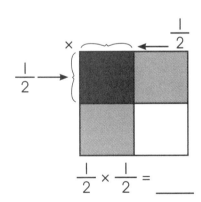

$$\frac{1}{2} \times \frac{1}{2} = \underline{\hspace{1cm}}$$

D.

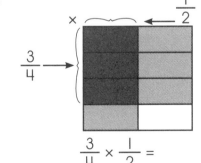

$$\frac{3}{4} \times \frac{1}{2} = \underline{\hspace{1cm}}$$

 MATH SUCCESS RB-904107

MULTIPLYING FRACTIONS

When multiplying $\frac{1}{2} \times \frac{1}{4}$:

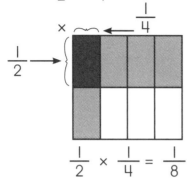

$$\frac{1}{2} \times \frac{1}{4} = \frac{1}{8}$$

1. Multiply the numerators.
2. Multiply the denominators.

$$\frac{1}{2} \times \frac{1}{4} = \frac{1 \times 1}{2 \times 4} = \frac{1}{8}$$

$$\frac{3}{4} \times \frac{1}{7} = \frac{1 \times 3}{4 \times 7} = \frac{3}{28}$$

Solve each problem.

A. $\frac{1}{2} \times \frac{3}{4} =$ $\frac{2}{3} \times \frac{1}{5} =$ $\frac{2}{5} \times \frac{1}{3} =$ $\frac{5}{6} \times \frac{1}{2} =$

B. $\frac{1}{4} \times \frac{3}{8} =$ $\frac{5}{12} \times \frac{1}{2} =$ $\frac{1}{2} \times \frac{5}{7} =$ $\frac{1}{3} \times \frac{1}{4} =$

C. $\frac{1}{5} \times \frac{2}{5} =$ $\frac{3}{5} \times \frac{1}{2} =$ $\frac{3}{4} \times \frac{3}{5} =$ $\frac{3}{4} \times \frac{1}{8} =$

D. $\frac{2}{5} \times \frac{3}{5} =$ $\frac{1}{2} \times \frac{1}{2} =$ $\frac{2}{3} \times \frac{2}{3} =$ $\frac{3}{8} \times \frac{1}{2} =$

E. $\frac{5}{7} \times \frac{1}{3} =$ $\frac{1}{2} \times \frac{3}{7} =$ $\frac{5}{8} \times \frac{1}{3} =$ $\frac{5}{6} \times \frac{1}{3} =$

F. $\frac{3}{5} \times \frac{1}{7} =$ $\frac{1}{8} \times \frac{1}{2} =$ $\frac{1}{4} \times \frac{3}{7} =$ $\frac{5}{9} \times \frac{1}{2} =$

MULTIPLYING FRACTIONS

$$\frac{1}{3} \times \frac{3}{8} = \frac{1 \times 3}{3 \times 8}$$

$$= \frac{3}{24}$$

$$= \frac{1}{8}$$

When multiplying fractions:
1. Multiply the numerators.
2. Multiply the denominators.
3. Simplify if possible.

$$\frac{3}{4} \times \frac{4}{5} = \frac{3 \times 4}{4 \times 5}$$

$$= \frac{12}{20}$$

$$= \frac{3}{5}$$

Solve each problem. Simplify if possible.

A. $\frac{3}{8} \times \frac{2}{3} =$ $\frac{4}{5} \times \frac{1}{2} =$ $\frac{1}{3} \times \frac{6}{7} =$ $\frac{1}{2} \times \frac{4}{7} =$

B. $\frac{2}{3} \times \frac{5}{6} =$ $\frac{1}{3} \times \frac{3}{10} =$ $\frac{4}{9} \times \frac{3}{4} =$ $\frac{5}{6} \times \frac{3}{10} =$

C. $\frac{3}{8} \times \frac{1}{6} =$ $\frac{2}{3} \times \frac{6}{7} =$ $\frac{5}{6} \times \frac{1}{10} =$ $\frac{3}{8} \times \frac{4}{9} =$

D. $\frac{3}{10} \times \frac{5}{8} =$ $\frac{3}{5} \times \frac{2}{9} =$ $\frac{3}{7} \times \frac{2}{3} =$ $\frac{2}{3} \times \frac{1}{4} =$

MATH SUCCESS RB-904107   © Rainbow Bridge Publishing

MULTIPLYING FRACTIONS BY WHOLE NUMBERS

When multiplying a whole number and a fraction:

$8 \times \dfrac{3}{8} = \dfrac{8}{1} \times \dfrac{3}{8}$

$\qquad = \dfrac{8 \times 3}{1 \times 8}$

$\qquad = \dfrac{24}{8}$

$\qquad = \mathbf{3}$

1. Rewrite the whole number as a fraction. (Write a denominator of 1.)
2. Multiply the numerators.
3. Multiply the denominators.
4. Simplify if possible.

$\dfrac{3}{4} \times 6 = \dfrac{3}{4} \times \dfrac{6}{1}$

$\qquad = \dfrac{3 \times 6}{4 \times 1}$

$\qquad = \dfrac{18}{4}$

$\qquad = 4\dfrac{2}{4} = \mathbf{4\dfrac{1}{2}}$

Solve each problem. Simplify if possible.

A. $\quad 3 \times \dfrac{2}{3} =$ $\qquad \dfrac{4}{5} \times 2 =$ $\qquad 1 \times \dfrac{6}{7} =$ $\qquad 2 \times \dfrac{4}{7} =$

B. $\quad \dfrac{2}{5} \times 6 =$ $\qquad 3 \times \dfrac{3}{10} =$ $\qquad 9 \times \dfrac{3}{4} =$ $\qquad 6 \times \dfrac{3}{10} =$

C. $\quad 8 \times \dfrac{1}{6} =$ $\qquad 2 \times \dfrac{6}{7} =$ $\qquad 6 \times \dfrac{1}{10} =$ $\qquad \dfrac{3}{8} \times 4 =$

D. $\quad \dfrac{3}{10} \times 5 =$ $\qquad 5 \times \dfrac{2}{9} =$ $\qquad \dfrac{3}{7} \times 2 =$ $\qquad \dfrac{2}{3} \times 4 =$

MULTIPLYING MIXED NUMBERS BY FRACTIONS

When multiplying a mixed number and a fraction:

$$2\frac{1}{3} \times \frac{4}{5} = \frac{7}{3} \times \frac{4}{5}$$

1. Rewrite the mixed number as an improper fraction.

$$\frac{1}{3} \times 2\frac{2}{3} = \frac{1}{3} \times \frac{8}{3}$$

$$= \frac{7 \times 4}{3 \times 5}$$

2. Multiply the numerators.

$$= \frac{1 \times 8}{3 \times 3}$$

3. Multiply the denominators.

$$= \frac{28}{15}$$

4. Simplify if possible.

$$= \frac{8}{9}$$

$$= 1\frac{13}{15}$$

Solve each problem. Simplify if possible.

A. $\frac{1}{2} \times 1\frac{1}{8} =$ $2\frac{1}{3} \times \frac{1}{3} =$ $4\frac{1}{2} \times \frac{1}{3} =$ $2\frac{2}{3} \times \frac{3}{7} =$

B. $3\frac{1}{2} \times \frac{1}{4} =$ $\frac{3}{5} \times 3\frac{1}{2} =$ $\frac{2}{5} \times 3\frac{1}{3} =$ $\frac{2}{3} \times 5\frac{1}{4} =$

C. $4\frac{3}{4} \times \frac{1}{3} =$ $\frac{1}{9} \times 2\frac{1}{2} =$ $\frac{1}{2} \times 1\frac{3}{5} =$ $\frac{1}{6} \times 3\frac{1}{3} =$

D. $4\frac{2}{3} \times \frac{3}{4} =$ $9\frac{1}{2} \times \frac{1}{6} =$ $3\frac{3}{4} \times \frac{5}{12} =$ $2\frac{1}{3} \times \frac{3}{8} =$

MULTIPLYING MIXED NUMBERS BY WHOLE NUMBERS

When multiplying a mixed number and a whole number:

$2\frac{1}{3} \times 4 = \frac{7}{3} \times \frac{4}{1}$

$= \frac{7 \times 4}{3 \times 1}$

$= \frac{28}{3}$

$= \mathbf{9\frac{1}{3}}$

1. Rewrite the numbers as improper fractions.
2. Multiply the numerators.
3. Multiply the denominators.
4. Simplify if possible.

$6 \times 3\frac{2}{3} = \frac{6}{1} \times \frac{11}{3}$

$= \frac{6 \times 11}{1 \times 3}$

$= \frac{66}{3}$

$= \mathbf{22}$

Solve each problem. Simplify if possible.

A. $3\frac{1}{4} \times 2 =$ $1\frac{4}{5} \times 2 =$ $1 \times 3\frac{6}{7} =$ $2 \times 4\frac{4}{7} =$

B. $3\frac{2}{5} \times 2 =$ $3 \times 2\frac{3}{10} =$ $9 \times 1\frac{3}{4} =$ $3 \times 4\frac{3}{10} =$

C. $3 \times 4\frac{1}{6} =$ $2 \times 3\frac{6}{7} =$ $6 \times 2\frac{1}{10} =$ $5\frac{3}{8} \times 4 =$

D. $2\frac{3}{10} \times 4 =$ $5 \times 2\frac{5}{9} =$ $5\frac{1}{7} \times 2 =$ $6\frac{2}{3} \times 4 =$

MATH SUCCESS RB-904107

MULTIPLYING MIXED NUMBERS

When multiplying mixed numbers:

$$2\frac{1}{4} \times 1\frac{1}{2} = \frac{9}{4} \times \frac{3}{2}$$

$$= \frac{9 \times 3}{4 \times 2}$$

$$= \frac{27}{8}$$

$$= \mathbf{3\frac{3}{8}}$$

1. Rewrite the numbers as improper fractions.
2. Multiply the numerators.
3. Multiply the denominators.
4. Simplify if possible.

$$1\frac{1}{3} \times 2\frac{1}{8} = \frac{4}{3} \times \frac{17}{8}$$

$$= \frac{4 \times 17}{3 \times 8}$$

$$= \frac{68}{24}$$

$$= 2\frac{20}{24} = \mathbf{2\frac{5}{6}}$$

Solve each problem. Simplify if possible.

A.　　$3\frac{3}{4} \times 2\frac{2}{3} =$　　　$1\frac{1}{4} \times 2\frac{1}{2} =$　　　$2\frac{1}{5} \times 2\frac{1}{4} =$　　　$1\frac{1}{5} \times 2\frac{1}{6} =$

B.　　$1\frac{3}{5} \times 1\frac{2}{5} =$　　　$2\frac{1}{2} \times 3\frac{1}{3} =$　　　$4\frac{1}{2} \times 1\frac{2}{3} =$　　　$2\frac{4}{5} \times 5\frac{1}{4} =$

C.　　$2\frac{3}{8} \times 2\frac{1}{3} =$　　　$1\frac{4}{5} \times 1\frac{1}{4} =$　　　$1\frac{3}{7} \times 1\frac{3}{8} =$　　　$1\frac{1}{2} \times 3\frac{2}{3} =$

D.　　$4\frac{1}{2} \times 1\frac{2}{5} =$　　　$2\frac{2}{3} \times 1\frac{1}{2} =$　　　$4\frac{1}{2} \times 1\frac{1}{2} =$　　　$2\frac{3}{8} \times 3\frac{2}{7} =$

MATH SUCCESS RB-904107　　　© Rainbow Bridge Publishing

MULTIPLYING FRACTIONS BY WHOLE NUMBERS AND MIXED NUMBERS

Solve each problem. Simplify if possible.

A. $\dfrac{3}{4} \times \dfrac{1}{2} =$ $\dfrac{1}{3} \times \dfrac{2}{5} =$ $\dfrac{4}{5} \times \dfrac{1}{3} =$ $\dfrac{5}{8} \times \dfrac{3}{4} =$

B. $\dfrac{2}{3} \times \dfrac{3}{5} =$ $\dfrac{4}{5} \times \dfrac{5}{9} =$ $\dfrac{3}{8} \times \dfrac{4}{5} =$ $\dfrac{1}{5} \times \dfrac{10}{11} =$

C. $6 \times \dfrac{1}{3} =$ $5 \times \dfrac{1}{2} =$ $\dfrac{2}{3} \times 8 =$ $\dfrac{4}{5} \times 7 =$

D. $\dfrac{2}{3} \times 1\dfrac{1}{2} =$ $1\dfrac{4}{5} \times \dfrac{1}{3} =$ $2\dfrac{1}{4} \times \dfrac{1}{3} =$ $3\dfrac{3}{4} \times \dfrac{1}{2} =$

E. $2\dfrac{3}{4} \times 5 =$ $2 \times 1\dfrac{1}{2} =$ $5 \times 2\dfrac{1}{5} =$ $1\dfrac{1}{3} \times 4 =$

MULTIPLYING FRACTIONS PROBLEM SOLVING

Solve each problem. Simplify if possible.

A. Austin wanted to go to the movie theater. It is $3\frac{3}{5}$ miles from his house. Austin decided to take his motor scooter, but it broke down $\frac{2}{3}$ of the way there. How far was Austin from his house?

_____

B. Austin's motor scooter uses $\frac{1}{4}$ of a gallon of fuel for each mile. How much fuel did he use? (Hint: Use your answer from Question A.)

_____

C. Austin purchased $\frac{2}{3}$ of a pound of yum-yum treats. If yum-yum treats are $6.00 per pound, how much did Austin pay?

_____

D. At the theater, Austin met his friends, who had purchased 1 large popcorn. Only $\frac{3}{4}$ of it was left. Austin ate $\frac{1}{3}$ of what was left. How much of the popcorn did Austin eat?

_____

E. After the movie, Austin started walking home. He walked $\frac{1}{6}$ of the $3\frac{3}{5}$ miles to his house before his mom picked him up. How far did Austin walk?

_____

F. Each night, Austin goes to bed and sleeps for an average of $8\frac{2}{3}$ hours. In one week, how many hours of sleep does Austin get?

_____

MULTIPLYING FRACTIONS PROBLEM SOLVING

Solve each problem. Simplify if possible.

A. Jacob's class has 24 students. If $\frac{1}{8}$ of them play the piano, how many students in his class play the piano?

B. There are 12 students working in the library. If $\frac{3}{4}$ of them are girls, how many girls are in the library?

C. Six students are working on math. Two-thirds of them are working on fractions. How many students are working on fractions?

D. Jacob's gym class lasts for $1\frac{1}{2}$ hours. He jumped rope for $\frac{1}{2}$ of that time. How long did he spend jumping rope?

E. Jacob's class spent $1\frac{3}{4}$ hours in science class. Two-thirds of the time was spent studying insects. How much time did he spend studying insects?

F. There are 20 students at lunch. One-fifth of the students are in the hall. How many students are in the hall?

MATH SUCCESS RB-904107

99

Solve each problem. Simplify if possible.

A. $\dfrac{4}{5} \times \dfrac{1}{3} =$ $\dfrac{4}{11} \times \dfrac{2}{3} =$ $\dfrac{1}{2} \times \dfrac{6}{11} =$ $\dfrac{4}{7} \times \dfrac{5}{6} =$

B. $7 \times \dfrac{3}{4} =$ $6 \times \dfrac{3}{10} =$ $\dfrac{2}{3} \times 1\dfrac{4}{5} =$ $\dfrac{5}{6} \times 1\dfrac{3}{4} =$

C. $3 \times 2\dfrac{1}{3} =$ $5 \times 1\dfrac{1}{2} =$ $6 \times 1\dfrac{2}{3} =$ $2 \times \dfrac{5}{6} =$

D. $2\dfrac{1}{2} \times 1\dfrac{3}{4} =$ $1\dfrac{1}{2} \times 2\dfrac{2}{3} =$ $4\dfrac{2}{3} \times 1\dfrac{4}{5} =$ $2\dfrac{3}{5} \times 2\dfrac{5}{6} =$

E.   If Laura reads $1\dfrac{1}{3}$ hours a week, how many total hours will she read in 5 weeks?

F.   Mike uses $2\dfrac{3}{4}$ cups of oats in each batch of cookies that he bakes. How many cups of oats will he use if he bakes 3 batches of cookies?

Solve each problem. Simplify if possible.

A. $\dfrac{1}{4} \times \dfrac{5}{6} =$ $\dfrac{7}{10} \times \dfrac{1}{3} =$ $\dfrac{3}{7} \times \dfrac{1}{6} =$ $\dfrac{9}{10} \times \dfrac{5}{12} =$

B. $8 \times \dfrac{3}{4} =$ $4 \times \dfrac{5}{12} =$ $\dfrac{2}{3} \times 2\dfrac{4}{7} =$ $3\dfrac{1}{8} \times \dfrac{2}{3} =$

C. $\dfrac{5}{6} \times 2\dfrac{1}{4} =$ $1 \times 3\dfrac{2}{3} =$ $5 \times 1\dfrac{1}{4} =$ $6 \times 2\dfrac{3}{4} =$

D. $2 \times 3\dfrac{4}{9} =$ $2\dfrac{1}{3} \times 2\dfrac{3}{4} =$ $1\dfrac{1}{5} \times 1\dfrac{2}{3} =$ $3\dfrac{2}{5} \times 1\dfrac{2}{3} =$

E. For 16 days, Zoe practiced the piano for $\dfrac{3}{4}$ an hour each day. What is the total time that Zoe spent practicing the piano?

F. Jake rides his bicycle $\dfrac{1}{4}$ mile to and from school for 6 days in the month of September. How many miles did Jake ride his bicycle in September?

READING DECIMALS

Just like there are place value names for numbers larger than 0, there are also names for place values after the decimal point.

thousands	hundreds	tens	ones	.	tenths	hundredths	thousandths
1	2	4	5	.	1	7	6

Decimal	Read As	Equivalent Fraction
0.7	seven tenths	$\frac{7}{10}$
0.23	twenty-three hundredths	$\frac{23}{100}$
0.045	forty-five thousandths	$\frac{45}{1000}$
15.01	fifteen and one hundredth	$15\frac{1}{100}$

Hint: "and" separates the whole number from the fraction.

Fill in each blank with the correct equivalent.

	Decimal	Read As	Equivalent Fraction
A.	0.3	three-tenths	_____
B.	1.12	_____	_____
C.	_____	two hundred twenty-one thousandths	_____
D.	_____	_____	$\frac{53}{100}$
E	0.871	_____	
F.	_____	_____	$\frac{5}{100}$
G.	0.783	_____	_____
H.	_____	two and six tenths	_____
I.	_____	_____	$\frac{115}{1000}$

EQUIVALENT DECIMALS AND FRACTIONS

Study how to rewrite decimals and fractions.

$$\frac{4}{10} = 0.4 \qquad\qquad 5.78 = 5\frac{78}{100}$$

$$5\frac{874}{1000} = 5.874 \qquad\qquad 1.521 = 1\frac{521}{1000}$$

Write each fraction or mixed number as a decimal.

A. $5\frac{78}{100} =$ 　　　　　　　　　$\frac{23}{100} =$

B. $1\frac{3}{100} =$ 　　　　　　　　　$\frac{5}{10} =$

C. $\frac{548}{1000} =$ 　　　　　　　　　$2\frac{53}{100} =$

D. $53\frac{17}{100} =$ 　　　　　　　　$16\frac{303}{1000} =$

E. $\frac{91}{1000} =$ 　　　　　　　　　$91\frac{3}{10} =$

Write each decimal as a mixed number or fraction.

F. 2.87 = 　　　　　　　　　0.983 =

G. 14.5 = 　　　　　　　　　287.69 =

H. 1.752 = 　　　　　　　　0.7 =

I. 0.06 = 　　　　　　　　　10.054 =

J. 81.2 = 　　　　　　　　　0.157 =

VISUALIZING DECIMALS

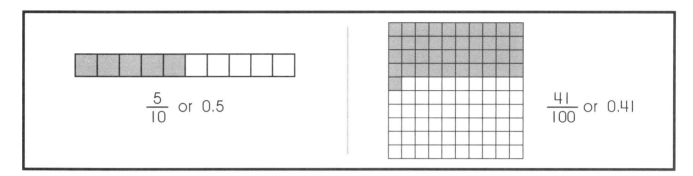

$\dfrac{5}{10}$ or 0.5

$\dfrac{41}{100}$ or 0.41

Write the fraction and decimal for each figure.

	Fraction	**Decimal**

A.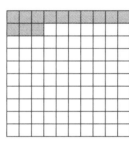

_____   _____

B.

_____   _____

C.

_____   _____

D.

_____   _____

E.

_____   _____

F.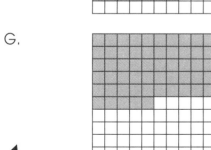

_____   _____

G.

_____   _____

MATH SUCCESS RB-904107

COMPARING DECIMALS

Comparing decimals is similar to comparing whole numbers.
 1. Line up the numbers by place value.
 2. Compare the digits left to right.

Example 1: 0.08 ☐ 0.8

 1. Line up: 0.08
              0.8
 2. Compare.
    After the decimal points, you have 0 and 8. 8 is bigger than 0, so 0.8 is bigger.

0.08 < 0.8

Example 2: 11.13 ☐ 11.03

11.13
11.03

The 11s before the decimal points are the same. After the decimal points, you have 1 and 0. Which is bigger? 1 is.

11.13 > 11.03

Use >, <, or = to compare each pair of decimals.

A. 0.007 ☐ 0.07   0.04 ☐ 0.4   2.159 ☐ 2.259

B. 101.05 ☐ 101.005   10.05 ☐ 10.005   9.50 ☐ 7.05

C. 0.99 ☐ 0.009   214.01 ☐ 214.001 30.249 ☐ 30.429

D. 9.008 ☐ 9.08   0.004 ☐ 4.00   614.05 ☐ 614.05

E. 6.041 ☐ 6.401   8.26 ☐ 8.026   92.001 ☐ 92.001

F. 43.014 ☐ 43.104   263.08 ☐ 263.81   0.83 ☐ 0.63

COMPARING AND ORDERING DECIMALS

Write the prices on the menu in order from least to greatest.

A. $1.25 $2.03 $1.07 $2.51 $1.10 $2.15 $2.21 $1.05

Item:	Price:
Soda	
Milk	
Fries	
Salad	
Cheese Sandwich	
Tuna Sandwich	
Hamburger	
Cheeseburger	

Circle the largest decimal in each row.

B. 4.05   4.50   4.005   4.15   4.55   4.5

C. 10.57   10.49   10.005   10.057   10.75   10.094

D. 2.5   2.15   2.52   2.005   2.095   2.51

E. 1.8   1.84   1.48   1.847   1.75   1.5

F. 89.90   88.19   8.90   89.09   89.5   89.01

STANDARD LENGTH

I foot (ft.) = 12 inches (in.) I yard (yd.) = 3 feet (ft.) I mile (mi.) = 5,280 feet (ft.)	
To convert a smaller unit to a larger unit, divide.	To convert a larger unit to a smaller unit, multiply.
48 in. = _____ ft. if 12 in. = 1 ft. then 48 in. = (48 ÷ 12) ft. = 4 ft. 48 in. = __4__ ft.	3 ft. = _____ in. if 1 ft. = 12 in. then 3 ft. = (3 x 12) in. = 36 in. 3 ft. = __36__ in.

Circle the best answer.

A. The length of a desk   3 in.   3 ft.   3 yd.   3 mi.

B. The length of a pencil   8 in.   8 ft.   8 yd.   8 mi.

C. The height of a school   7 in.   7 ft.   7 yd.   7 mi.

Convert each measurement.

D. 60 in. = _____ ft.   5 ft. = _____ in.

E. 4 yd. 2 ft. = _____ ft.   2 mi. = _____ ft.

F. 7 ft. 3 in. = _____ in.   3 mi. 310 ft. = _____ ft.

G. 13 ft. 2 in. = _____ in.   21 yd. 6 ft. = _____ ft.

Solve each problem.

H. Gabriel ran for 1 mile. Then, he started jogging. He jogged for 250 feet. How many total feet did he run and jog?

I. Derek has 2 feet of Tasty Cherry Rope. He plans on splitting it evenly between himself and 5 of his friends. How many inches should each person get?

METRIC LENGTH

> **1 kilometer (km) = 1,000 meters (m)**
> **1 meter (m) = 100 centimeters (cm)**
> **1 centimeter (cm) = 10 millimeters (mm)**
>
> 1 meter (m) is about the length of a baseball bat.
>
> ←—— 1 meter ——→
>
>
> 1 centimeter (cm) is about the width of your index finger.
>
>  ←— 1 centimeter
>
> 1 millimeter (mm) is about the width of a head on a pin.
>
> 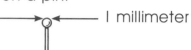 ←— 1 millimeter
>
> 1 kilometer (km) is just over $\frac{1}{2}$ a mile.
>
> ←—— 1 kilometer ——→
>

Circle the best answer.

A. height of a house   11 m   11 cm

B. What would you measure the height of a tree in?   mm   cm   m   km

C. What would you measure the length of a spoon in?   mm   cm   m   km

Convert each measurement.

D. 42 m = _____ cm   4 km = _____ m   85 cm = _____ mm

Solve each problem.

E. Dylan has a roll of wrapping paper that is 5 meters long. How many centimeters of wrapping paper does he have?

F. The Kilgore family traveled 35,000 meters to get to the nearest amusement park. How many kilometers did they have to travel?

MATH SUCCESS RB-904107

STANDARD CAPACITY AND MASS

I pint (pt.) = 2 cups (c.)
I quart (qt.) = 2 pints (pt.)
I gallon (gal.) = 4 quarts (qt.)
I pound (lb.) = 16 ounces (oz.)

3 pt. = _____ cups

if I pt. = 2 cups

then
3 pt. = (3 x 2) cups = 6 cups

3 pt. = __**6**__ cups

38 qt. = _____ gal.

if 4 qt. = I gal.

then
8 qt. = (8 ÷ 4) gal. = 2 gal.

8 qt. = __**2**__ gal.

Circle the best answer.

A. the capacity of a glass   2 cups   2 pt.   2 qt.   2 gal.

B. the capacity of a tub   60 cups   60 pt.   60 qt.   60 gal.

C. the capacity of a sink   2 cups   2 pt.   2 qt.   2 gal.

D. the capacity of a pitcher   2 cups   2 pt.   2 qt.   2 gal.

Convert each measurement.

E. 5 pt. = _____ cups   4 pt. = _____ qt.

F. 2 qt. = _____ pt.   32 oz. = _____ lb.

G. 3 gal. = _____ qt.   8 cups = _____ pt.

H. 5 lb. 8 oz. = _____ oz.   4 pt. I cup = _____ cups

I. 4 qt. I pt. = _____ pt.   16 qt. = _____ gal.

J. 5 pt. I cup = _____ cups   12 pt. = _____ cups

K. 22 pt. = _____ qt.   8 lb. 7 oz. = _____ oz.

L. 14 qt. I pt. = _____ pt.   20 cups = _____ pt.

MATH SUCCESS RB-904107

METRIC CAPACITY AND MASS

---

1 kiloliter (kL) = 1,000 liters (L)
1 liter (L) = 1,000 milliliters (mL)

1 kiloliter (kL) is equal to 1,000 liters. It would take 500 2-liter soft drink bottles to equal one kiloliter.

7 kL = _____ L
Think: 1 kL = 1,000 L
So, 7 kL = (7 x 1,000) L
7 kL = **7,000 L**

1 milliliter (mL) is very small. It is about $\frac{1}{5}$ of a teaspoon.

8,000 mL = _____ L
Think: 1,000 mL = 1 L
So, 8,000 mL = (8,000 ÷ 1,000) L
8,000 mL = **8 L**

Circle the best answer.

A. capacity of a gallon of milk   3.8 mL   3.8 L

B. one teaspoon of vanilla   5 mL   5 L

C. five bathtubs of water   100 L   1 kL

D. dropper of medicine   1 mL   1 L

Convert each measurement.

E. 2 kL = _____ L   5 L = _____ mL   24 kL = _____ L

F. 2,000 mL = _____ L   45,000 L = _____ kL   38 L = _____ mL

The word *mass* is similar to the word *weight*.

1 gram (g) is about the mass of a dollar bill.

1,000 grams (g) = 1 kilogram (kg)

Kilograms (kg) are used to measure the mass of larger objects. A newborn baby usually weighs 3 to 4 kilograms.

Circle the best answer.

G. a sack of potatoes   5 kg   5 g

H. one teaspoon of vanilla   5 mL   5 L

Convert each measurement.

I. 7 kg = _____ g   6,000 g = _____ kg   73,000 g = _____ kg

J. A cat weighs 4 kilograms. How many grams does it weigh? _____

110

PERIMETER

Perimeter (P) is the distance around a figure.

Perimeter = 2 + 5 + 2 + 5
P = **14 cm**

Perimeter = 2.5 + 2.5 + 3.5
P = **8.5 cm**

Measure the length of each side to find each shape's perimeter in centimeters.

A.

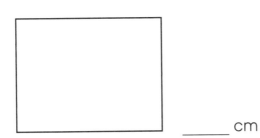 _____ cm

_____ cm

B.

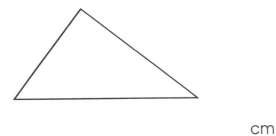 _____ cm

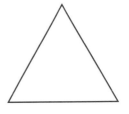 _____ cm

C.

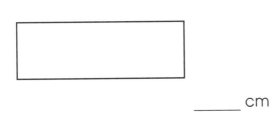 _____ cm

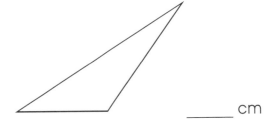 _____ cm

MATH SUCCESS RB-904107

PERIMETER

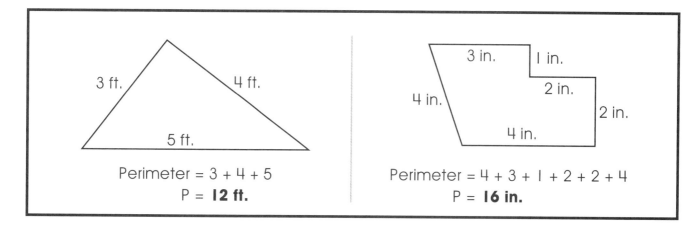

Perimeter = 3 + 4 + 5
P = **12 ft.**

Perimeter = 4 + 3 + 1 + 2 + 2 + 4
P = **16 in.**

Find the perimeter of each object.

A.

4 yd.

2 yd.   2 yd.

4 yd.   _____ yd.

B.

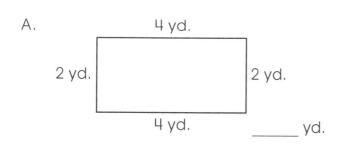

6 ft.   10 ft.

8 ft.

_____ ft.

C.

1 ft.

1 ft.

5 ft.   _____ ft.

D.

3 yd.   3 yd.

3 yd.   3 yd.

_____ yd.

E.

8 in.

6 in.

6 in.   7 in.

8 in.   _____ in.

F.

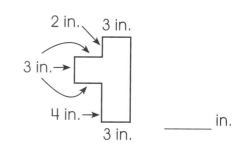

2 in.   3 in.

3 in. →

4 in. →

3 in.   _____ in.

AREA

The **area** of a rectangle is equal to its length times its width.

4 cm

2 cm

$A = l \times w$

$Area = 4 \times 2$

A = 8 cm²

Find the area of each object.

A.   4 ft.

3 ft.

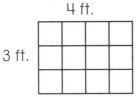

_____ ft.²

B.   5 m

5 m

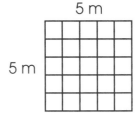

_____ m²

C.   10 km

2 km

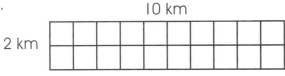

_____ km²

D.   12 in.

7 in.

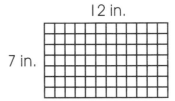

_____ in.²

Fill in each blank.

	Length	Width	Area
E.	3 feet	6 feet	_____ ft.²
F.	1 inch	_____ inches	4 in.²
G.	5 cm	6 cm	_____ cm²
H.	3 km	5 km	_____ km²
I.	4 mm	_____ mm	20 mm²

MATH SUCCESS RB-904107

LINES

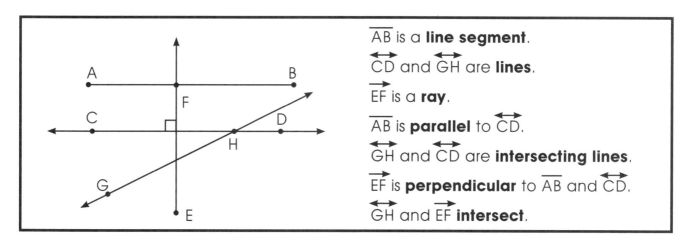

$\overline{AB}$ is a **line segment**.

$\overleftrightarrow{CD}$ and $\overleftrightarrow{GH}$ are **lines**.

$\overrightarrow{EF}$ is a **ray**.

$\overline{AB}$ is **parallel** to $\overleftrightarrow{CD}$.

$\overleftrightarrow{GH}$ and $\overleftrightarrow{CD}$ are **intersecting lines**.

$\overrightarrow{EF}$ is **perpendicular** to $\overline{AB}$ and $\overleftrightarrow{CD}$.

$\overleftrightarrow{GH}$ and $\overrightarrow{EF}$ **intersect**.

Circle the best answer.

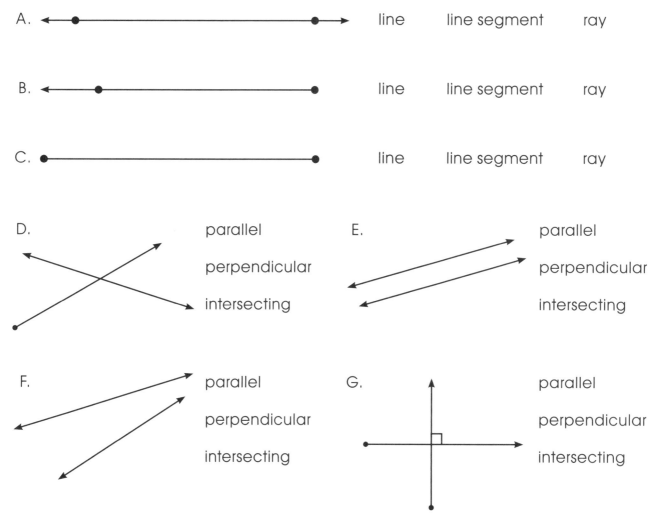

A.   line   line segment   ray

B.   line   line segment   ray

C.   line   line segment   ray

D.   parallel   perpendicular   intersecting

E.   parallel   perpendicular   intersecting

F.   parallel   perpendicular   intersecting

G.   parallel   perpendicular   intersecting

ANGLES

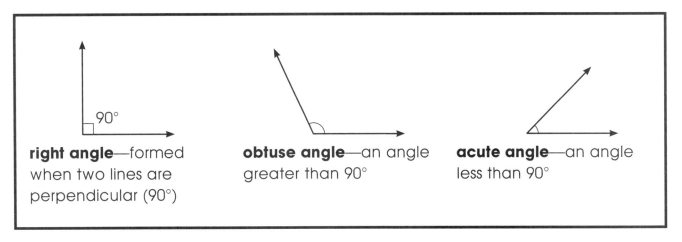

right angle—formed when two lines are perpendicular (90°)

obtuse angle—an angle greater than 90°

acute angle—an angle less than 90°

Name the type of angle shown.

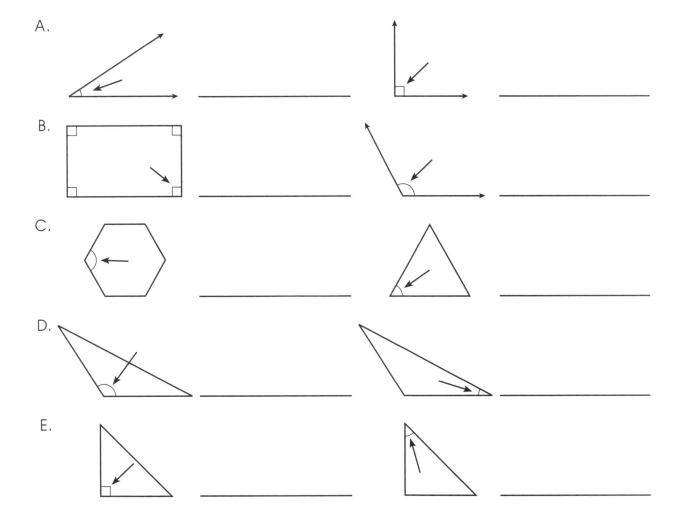

A. _____   _____

B. _____   _____

C. _____   _____

D. _____   _____

E. _____   _____

MATH SUCCESS RB-904107

POLYGONS

Some polygons have more than one classification. These are the general names of polygons, named for the number of sides.

triangle = 3 sides   quadrilateral = 4 sides   pentagon = 5 sides   hexagon = 6 sides   heptagon = 7 sides   octagon = 8 sides

Name the type of polygon shown.

A.
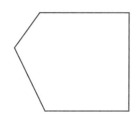
_____

B.
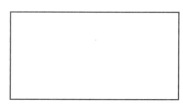
_____

C.
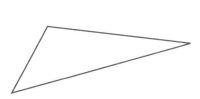
_____

D.
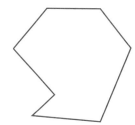
_____

E.
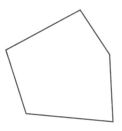
_____

F.
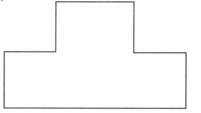
_____

CONGRUENT AND SIMILAR

Congruent polygons have equal side lengths and angles.
Similar polygons have equal angles.

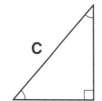

Parallelograms A and B
are **congruent**.

Triangles C and D
are **similar** triangles.

Classify each pair as *similar* or *congruent*.

A.

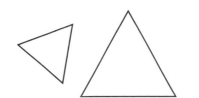

_____   _____

B.

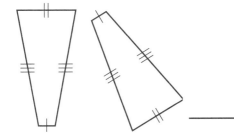   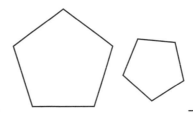

_____   _____

C.

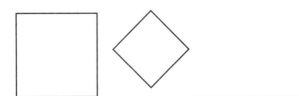   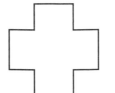

_____   _____

MATH SUCCESS RB-904107

117

GEOMETRIC SOLIDS

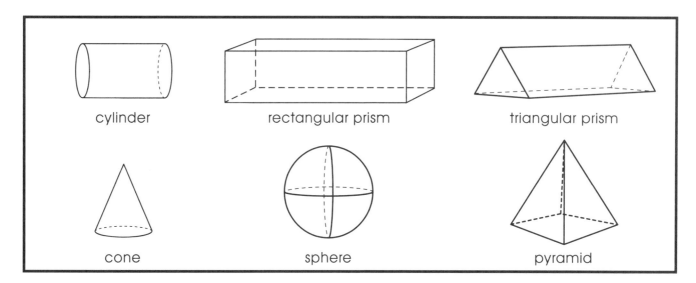

cylinder   rectangular prism   triangular prism

cone   sphere   pyramid

Name the type of figure shown.

A.

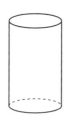 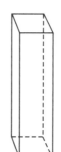

_____   _____

B.

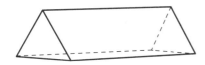 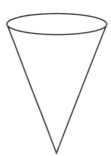

_____   _____

C.

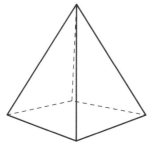 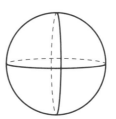

_____   _____

MATH SUCCESS RB-904107

GEOMETRIC SOLIDS

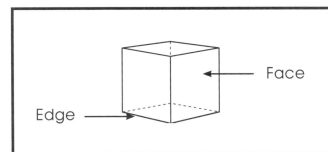

Face

Edge

A **face** is a flat surface.
A cube has 6 **faces** (sides).

An **edge** is a line segment where two faces meet. A cube has 12 **edges**.

Write the number of faces and edges for each figure.

	Faces	**Edges**

A.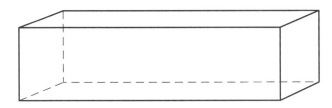

_____   _____

B.

_____   _____

C.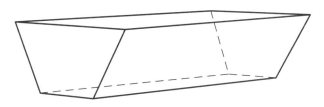

_____   _____

D.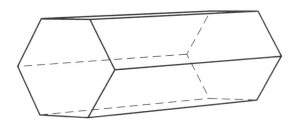

_____   _____

TRANSFORMATIONS

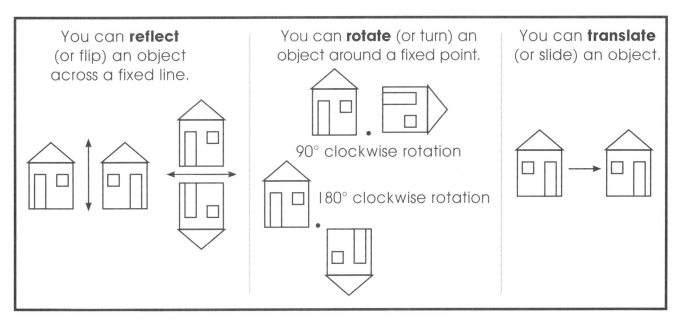

You can **reflect** (or flip) an object across a fixed line.

You can **rotate** (or turn) an object around a fixed point.

90° clockwise rotation

180° clockwise rotation

You can **translate** (or slide) an object.

Follow the directions to draw each new figure.

A. Reflect.

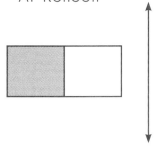

B. Rotate 90° clockwise.

C. Rotate 180° clockwise.

D. Translate.

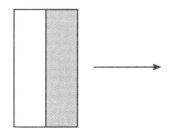

MATH SUCCESS RB-904107

ANSWER KEY

Page 4
A. 89; 42; 699; 820; 7,996;
B. $\frac{1}{4}$, $\frac{1}{2}$,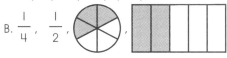

C. three-eighths, nine-halves, one-eighth;

D. 1, $\frac{5}{6}$, $\frac{2}{3}$, $\frac{5}{11}$, E. 3 ft.; F. 10 m

Page 5
A. 113; 39; 1,212; 93; 11,052; B. $7\frac{1}{2}$, $11\frac{1}{4}$, $4\frac{1}{8}$, $9\frac{2}{3}$;
C. $\frac{1}{2}$, $\frac{2}{3}$, $6\frac{1}{2}$, $5\frac{1}{4}$; D. $\frac{3}{8}$, $\frac{5}{18}$, $\frac{7}{8}$, $\frac{25}{108}$;
E. 5.78, 91.3, $81\frac{2}{10}$, $\frac{875}{1000}$

Page 6
A. 630; 1,544; 528; 11,232; 313,632; B. $1\frac{1}{2}$, $3\frac{7}{12}$, $3\frac{1}{4}$,
$2\frac{1}{5}$, $2\frac{2}{3}$; C. $\frac{27}{4}$, $\frac{8}{3}$, $\frac{10}{18}$, $\frac{42}{12}$; D. 12 qt., 24 cups,

5,000 mL; E. octagon, rectangular prism, pyramid

Page 7
A. 2; 9; 23; 2,432; B. $\frac{4}{6}$, $\frac{12}{15}$, $\frac{12}{20}$, $\frac{10}{12}$;
C. $\frac{3}{21}$, $\frac{14}{21}$, $\frac{4}{10}$, $\frac{5}{10}$, $\frac{15}{20}$, $\frac{4}{20}$; D. <, <; E. <, >;

F. acute, right; G. parallel, perpendicular

Page 8
A. 3 r1, 4 r13, 79, 211 r51; B. 2, $\frac{1}{8}$, $1\frac{1}{2}$; C. 9 slices;
D. $\frac{2}{5}$; E. 56 cm, 160 cm²; F. 54 in., 182 in.²

Page 10
A. 9, 17, 16, 14, 8, 9, 11; B. 5, 12, 14, 8, 18, 11, 4; C. 13, 12,
9, 16, 8, 11, 2; D. 5, 6, 4, 10, 15, 14, 13; E. 14, 6, 3, 7, 10,
11, 7; F. 12, 11, 6, 10, 11, 11, 13; G. 9, 14, 3, 13, 9, 8, 6;
H. 9, 12, 10, 18, 13, 10, 12; I. 12, 8, 10, 8, 9, 14, 10; J. 4, 15,
10, 5, 11, 12, 3

Page 11
A. 31, 97, 61, 53, 54, 87; B. 83, 74, 59, 56, 79, 91; C. 72, 95,
64, 47, 89, 99; D. 86, 56, 58, 99, 34, 39; E. 88, 95, 79, 89,
79, 52; F. 84, 69, 28, 59, 76, 89; G. 77, 46, 66, 66, 86, 77;
H. 88, 98, 78, 93, 81, 87

Page 12
A. 905; 894; 824; 1,170; 936; B. 1,298; 1,560; 1,003; 1,458;
899; C. 513; 873; 1,140; 1,324; 466; D. 678; 1,432; 776; 891;
1,031; E. 538; 595; 1,170; 1,639; 1,389; F. 1,145; 1,738; 539;
1,381; 385; G. 1,029; 865; 1,117; 1,153; 1,236

Page 13
A. 9,199; 12,788; 4,714; 12,471; 5,323; B. 10,347; 9,530;
14,552; 11,585; 10,966; C. 12,264; 11,319; 7,305; 8,567;
3,782; D. 12,731; 5,110; 7,536; 13,375; 8,031; E. 7,411;
18,264; 10,623; 8,037; 10,887; F. 89,562; 122,121; 93,467;
164,229; 79,387; G. 51,631; 157,245; 83,384; 61,133;
110,615

Page 14
A. 1,965; 2,381; 798; 789; 1,437; B. 15,301; 20,660; 13,608;
22,532; 13,031; C. 1,203; 23,745; 18,407; 125,172; 127,881;
D. 2,365; 2,446; 19,957; 28,793; 135,110

Page 15
A. 1, 5, 6, 3, 2, 7, 8, 1; B. 6, 1, 4, 2, 9, 9, 1, 0; C. 3, 6, 8, 5,
8, 7, 8, 8; D. 3, 8, 6, 4, 12, 7, 5, 3; E. 4, 1, 9, 2, 6, 8, 6, 9;
F. 9, 2, 3, 2, 1, 2, 5, 5; G. 1, 1, 4, 7, 9, 9, 3, 6; H. 7, 9, 9, 5, 6,
0, 3, 8; I. 0, 3, 4, 8, 8, 4, 5, 0; J. 2, 3, 1, 4, 4, 7, 2, 7

Page 16
A. 66, 14, 42, 24, 34, 51; B. 41, 13, 40, 61, 13, 16; C. 30, 24,
29, 40, 31, 30; D. 2, 10, 30, 14, 51, 21; E. 22, 24, 51, 32, 30,
42; F. 72, 31, 21, 35, 31, 64; G. 34, 54, 13, 15, 21, 26

Page 17
A. 1, 68, 27, 37, 46, 37; B. 9, 25, 29, 49, 19, 8; C. 5, 6, 73,
26, 39, 4; D. 35, 19, 46, 8, 16, 9; E. 47, 2, 52, 44, 18, 29;
F. 36, 9, 8, 9, 15, 6; G. 43, 27, 9, 42, 57, 16

Page 18
A. 474, 252, 671, 499, 18, 81; B. 698, 85, 498, 414, 129,
547; C. 246, 589, 73, 9, 61, 708; D. 385, 128, 790, 389, 382,
125; E. 72, 79, 368, 8, 54, 96; F. 678, 74, 232, 347, 224, 87;
G. 153, 497, 236, 290, 511, 249

Page 19
A. 1,063; 6,684; 1,612; 538; 791; B. 5,325; 2,107; 3,449;
4,841; 3,997; C. 80,967; 78,112; 79,946; 92,290; 60,048;
D. 51,236; 61,911; 70,136; 31,726; 92,591; E. 4,399; 58,527;
32,813; 1,921; 44,633; F. 45,434; 21,434; 5,611; 4,462; 1,264

ANSWER KEY

Page 20
A. 2,233 seats; B. 263 people; C. 6,747 people;
D. 1,747 people; E. 1,593 people; F. 3,027 people

Page 21
A. 1,074 books; B. 2,131 books; C. 131 books;
D. 1,925 books; E. 2,718 books; F. no

Page 22
A. 84; 112; 1,077; 1,007; 10,013; B. 15,534; 177,487; 20,652;
24,519; 158,382; C. 12, 27, 414, 540, 402; D. 270; 3,861; 1,942;
52,004; 10,000; E. 1,313 strawberries; F. 170 raffle tickets

Page 23
A. 83; 131; 735; 1,031; 8,274; B. 14,158; 199,584; 1,560;
20,101; 111,705; C. 6, 22, 16, 155, 174; D. 46; 417; 5,405;
2,145; 2,898; E. 55,109; 84,418; 39,419; 21,112; 12,029;
F. 55 points; G. 68 cookies

Page 24
A. 0, 9, 45, 0, 56, 24, 48, 10; B. 12, 24, 40, 35, 21, 20, 18, 0;
C. 8, 7, 9, 40, 42, 30, 0, 32; D. 9, 0, 54, 72, 18, 49, 64, 0;
E. 45, 6, 28, 72, 0, 8, 24, 20; F. 0, 12, 24, 4, 15, 14, 40, 15;
G. 7, 27, 21, 18, 25, 28, 0, 6; H. 42, 12, 35, 16, 8, 27, 0, 30;
I. 4, 24, 20, 16, 3, 2, 72, 5; J. 6, 63, 81, 63, 32, 0, 5, 36

Page 25
A. 162, 210, 343, 95, 148, 624; B. 124, 810, 68, 37, 180, 126;
C. 60, 272, 333, 26, 125, 511; D. 144, 0, 320, 0, 49, 172;
E. 108, 0, 186, 136, 324, 210; F. 609, 0, 488, 432, 348, 10;
G. 504, 828, 225, 124, 630, 138; H. 250, 23, 82, 231, 102, 0

Page 26
A. 348; 649; 5,484; 4,315; 1,434; 2,464; B. 2,528; 2,994;
3,357; 2,922; 6,125; 4,040; C. 1,614; 1,996; 3,600; 2,120;
1,953; 1,203; D. 2,448; 1,718; 3,856; 4,590; 772; 1,584;
E. 4,886; 2,322; 1,195; 766; 3,177; 0; F. 1,656; 558; 6,657;
1,233; 2,832; 1,650

Page 27
A. 6,162; 1,122; 1,675; 6,486; 2,940; 1,798; B. 2,115; 1,760;
1,032; 2,208; 2,166; 5,742; C. 3,290; 3,104; 5,060; 3,519;
4,455; 1,586; D. 3,168; 1,314; 1,034; 4,900; 1,312; 2,200;
E. 551; 1,242; 1,980; 7,332; 4,794; 1,881; F. 3,750; 945;
4,599; 770; 9,506; 6,020

Page 28
A. 64,588; 10,833; 10,720; 8,928; 18,262; 5,180; B. 23,760;
7,956; 13,962; 9,243; 25,376; 18,391; C. 21,009; 29,700;
13,110; 17,346; 20,544; 6,474; D. 10,188; 51,996; 6,000;
58,644; 66,240; 14,355

Page 29
A. 816,775; 481,500; 593,568; 96,712; 75,168; B. 858,364;
108,934; 130,442; 355,008; 337,425; C. 1,992,711;
2,784,960; 1,660,811; 1,112,034; 2,487,657

Page 30
A. $24.00; B. $22.00; C. 4 pounds of nuts, $28.00;
D. $325.00; E. $186.00; F. 675 people

Page 31
A. 46 hours; B. 75 hours; C. 884 hours; D. 212 hours;
E. 1,217 hours; yes; F. 950 hours; fewer

Page 32
A. 21, 30, 135, 576, 144, 455; B. 2,075; 5,154; 1,425; 1,482;
5,096; 576; C. 19,874; 33,573; 525,866; 143,982; 36,990;
370,978; D. 561,476; 211,820; 2,827,576; 1,257,616;
1,238,512; 1,865,125; E. 473 words; F. 252 doughnuts

Page 33
A. 45, 21, 344, 304, 357, 78; B. 1,872; 4,753; 2,162; 480;
2,037; 4,554; C. 46,458; 39,196; 175,348; 117,348; 222,712;
139,125; D. 300,651; 6,203,709; 2,392,677; 1,681,688;
3,058,988; 606,825; E. 336 index card labels; F. 1,920 seeds

Page 34
A. 6, 5, 6, 2, 2, 4, 4; B. 2, 2, 1, 8, 5, 3, 9; C. 7, 2, 9, 7, 3, 0,
7; D. 1, 8, 9, 1, 4, 6, 5; E. 8, 5, 7, 8, 9, 4, 1; F. 0, 3, 7, 1, 7, 8,
6; G. 2, 6, 2, 7, 9, 2, 5; H. 9, 3, 2, 6, 3, 5, 9; I. 8, 5, 4, 1, 1, 4,
7; J. 4, 8, 9, 7, 8, 8, 5

Page 35
A. 7, 9, 4, 3, 1, 2; B. 2, 3, 7, 9, 6, 3; C. 9, 6, 4, 8, 1, 5;
D. 9, 0, 8, 4, 8, 2; E. 2, 7, 0, 2, 7, 1

Page 36
A. 16, 12, 23, 19, 33; B. 19, 11, 18, 12, 14; C. 13, 8, 29, 30,
21; D. 15, 6, 18, 12, 17; E. 12, 4, 66, 13, 11

Page 37
A. 120, 160, 28, 34, 282; B. 18, 38, 216, 51, 16; C. 112, 27,
154, 234, 102

 **MATH SUCCESS** RB-904107

ANSWER KEY

Page 38

A. 11 r3, 13 r1, 1 r7, 28 r1, 26 r2; B. 95 r2, 55 r3, 119 r2, 95 r1, 241 r1; C. 195 r2, 58 r3, 77 r5, 277 r1, 122 r1; D. 247 r2, 31 r2, 62 r1, 105 r6, 130 r4

Page 39

A. 31 r4, 20 r1, 207 r3, 55 r1, 116 r3; B. 84 r6, 166 r1, 111 r2, 153 r5, 317 r2; C. 1,168 r4; 4,642 r1; 969 r4; 372 r2; 189 r1

Page 40

A. 1,628 r5; 533 r3; 804 r1; 900 r1; 1,007 r1; B. 552 r2; 1,617 r3; 1,906 r2; 471 r4; 513 r1; C. 556 r2; 1,875 r3; 520 r1; 630 r6; 718 r1

Page 41

A. 2 r12, 2 r1, 1 r6, 2 r10, 1 r16; B. 2, 1 r8, 1 r10, 1 r1, 1; C. 3 r10, 4, 1 r1, 1 r8, 2 r8; D. 2 r6, 1 r7, 2 r5, 1 r2, 3 r10

Page 42

A. 8 r80, 40 r8, 16 r13, 4 r30, 2 r26; B. 54 r6, 41 r10, 7 r3, 7 r78, 4 r9; C. 4 r9, 6 r54, 3 r31, 8 r23, 1 r64

Page 43

A. 9 r27, 31 r15, 4 r22, 18 r19, 23 r11; B. 7 r2, 1 r61, 7 r82, 15 r35, 20 r15; C. 16 r8, 35 r12, 5 r54, 9 r28, 8 r17

Page 44

A. 13 r78, 52 r1, 92 r92, 46 r40; B. 83 r9, 69 r11, 91 r59, 79 r16; C. 55 r26, 262 r6, 91 r29, 161 r41

Page 45

A. 238 r26, 733 r6, 537 r42, 410 r7; B. 696 r18, 596 r9, 792 r12, 734 r48; 1,001 r28; 970 r20; 850 r15; 2,280 r14

Page 46

A. 222 r5, 140 r30, 120 r20, 72 r6; B. 282 r19, 25 r25, 537 r33, 713 r30; C. 544 r17, 160 r7, 211 r51, 42 r40

Page 47

A. 13 human years; B. 8 human years; C. 7 human years, 3; D. 8 human years, 8; E. 29 years old, 179 days; F. 2 years old, 121 days

Page 48

A. 61 lawns; B. 250 square feet; C. $13.00; D. $2.00; E. 144 hours, 12 hours; F. $15.00

Page 49

A. 24, 5 r4, 78 r4, 284; B. 602, 620, 4 r3, 647 r3; C. 3 r18, 9 r45, 37 r53, 220 r36; D. 37 r53; 100 r12; 1,879 r5; 1,444 r12; E. 28 containers; F. 31 groups

Page 50

A. 31, 19 r2, 62 r3, 137 r2; B. 1,472 r2; 905 r3; 3 r9; 6 r2; C. 3, 8 r18, 90 r77, 156 r3; D. 63 r40; 86 r70; 223 r29; 2,119 r6; E. 87 boxes, 10 brownies; F. 78 full boxes

Page 51

A. $\dfrac{3}{8}$, $\dfrac{5}{8}$, $\dfrac{4}{6}$, $\dfrac{2}{6}$, $\dfrac{4}{8}$, $\dfrac{4}{6}$, $\dfrac{5}{6}$, $\dfrac{1}{6}$

B. $\dfrac{1}{4}$, $\dfrac{3}{4}$, $\dfrac{2}{3}$, $\dfrac{1}{3}$, $\dfrac{1}{8}$, $\dfrac{7}{8}$, $\dfrac{6}{8}$, $\dfrac{2}{8}$

C. $\dfrac{3}{6}$, $\dfrac{3}{6}$, $\dfrac{1}{6}$, $\dfrac{5}{6}$, $\dfrac{2}{6}$, $\dfrac{4}{6}$, $\dfrac{4}{12}$, $\dfrac{8}{12}$

Page 52

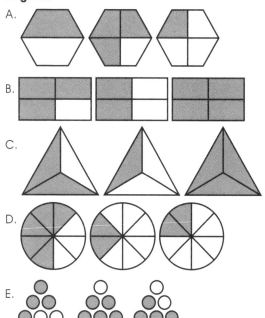

Page 53

A. $\dfrac{3}{5}$, $\dfrac{3}{4}$; B. $\dfrac{4}{9}$, $\dfrac{1}{4}$; C. $\dfrac{1}{3}$, $\dfrac{6}{12}$; D. $\dfrac{2}{8}$, $\dfrac{4}{10}$; E. $\dfrac{4}{5}$, $\dfrac{5}{11}$;

F. $\dfrac{1}{2}$, $\dfrac{7}{8}$; G. one-third, two-thirds; H. one-half, one-eighth;

I. three-eighths, four-elevenths; J. two-fifths, five-thirds;

K. five-sevenths, five-ninths; L. four-thirds, nine-halves

ANSWER KEY

Page 54

A. $7\frac{1}{2}$, $1\frac{3}{4}$, $2\frac{6}{7}$; B. $8\frac{3}{5}$, $2\frac{7}{8}$, $4\frac{1}{5}$; C. $2\frac{7}{12}$, $2\frac{1}{2}$, $1\frac{5}{8}$; D. $2\frac{3}{4}$, $5\frac{4}{9}$, $6\frac{5}{6}$; E. $7\frac{2}{3}$, $11\frac{1}{4}$, 12; F. $3\frac{2}{7}$, 12, 8

Page 55

A. $1\frac{1}{4}$, $3\frac{1}{2}$, $1\frac{1}{5}$; B. $2\frac{2}{3}$, $4\frac{1}{2}$, $2\frac{2}{5}$; C. $1\frac{4}{5}$, $8\frac{6}{7}$, $4\frac{2}{3}$; D. $2\frac{2}{5}$, 8, $7\frac{5}{12}$; E. $3\frac{1}{3}$, $7\frac{8}{9}$, $10\frac{1}{6}$; F. $6\frac{1}{2}$, $10\frac{4}{5}$, $1\frac{2}{7}$; G. $4\frac{1}{12}$, 10, $7\frac{5}{11}$; H. $3\frac{11}{12}$, $6\frac{4}{9}$, $9\frac{7}{10}$

Page 56

A. $\frac{7}{3}$, $\frac{27}{4}$, $\frac{13}{12}$; B. $\frac{25}{8}$, $\frac{38}{5}$, $\frac{19}{10}$; C. $\frac{17}{5}$, $\frac{103}{11}$, $\frac{27}{7}$; D. $\frac{29}{5}$, $\frac{53}{12}$, $\frac{73}{11}$

Page 57

A. $\frac{19}{5}$, $\frac{19}{8}$, $\frac{17}{12}$; B. $\frac{21}{8}$, $\frac{23}{4}$, $\frac{73}{9}$; C. $\frac{14}{3}$, $\frac{13}{2}$, $\frac{113}{9}$; D. $\frac{57}{8}$, $\frac{12}{7}$, $\frac{52}{11}$; E. $\frac{45}{7}$, $\frac{17}{5}$, $\frac{95}{12}$; F. $\frac{55}{8}$, $\frac{31}{12}$, $\frac{53}{10}$

Page 58

A. $\frac{1}{2}$, $\frac{2}{5}$, $\frac{1}{3}$; B. $\frac{2}{3}$, $\frac{1}{3}$, $\frac{3}{5}$; C. $\frac{3}{4}$, $\frac{1}{12}$, $\frac{2}{3}$; D. $\frac{1}{3}$, $\frac{1}{4}$, $\frac{5}{6}$; E. $\frac{1}{2}$, $\frac{1}{4}$, 1

Page 59

A. $\frac{1}{2}$, $\frac{5}{6}$, $\frac{1}{3}$; B. $\frac{5}{12}$, $\frac{1}{12}$, $\frac{2}{3}$; C. $\frac{2}{7}$, $\frac{1}{9}$, $\frac{1}{3}$; D. $\frac{1}{2}$, 1, $\frac{1}{3}$; E. $\frac{1}{3}$, $\frac{3}{5}$, $\frac{1}{2}$; F. $\frac{1}{3}$, $\frac{3}{4}$, $\frac{1}{8}$; G. $\frac{2}{3}$, $\frac{7}{20}$, $\frac{1}{2}$; H. $\frac{2}{5}$, $\frac{1}{3}$, $\frac{2}{3}$

Page 60

A. $2\frac{1}{2}$, $3\frac{1}{3}$, $2\frac{3}{4}$; B. $1\frac{2}{3}$, $6\frac{1}{2}$, 7; C. $2\frac{1}{4}$, $4\frac{1}{3}$, $6\frac{1}{2}$; D. 7, $5\frac{1}{4}$, $3\frac{1}{2}$

Page 61

A. $\frac{1}{3}$, $\frac{2}{3}$, $\frac{5}{6}$; B. $\frac{3}{4}$, $\frac{1}{6}$, $\frac{1}{2}$; C. $1\frac{1}{8}$, $2\frac{1}{5}$, $2\frac{2}{3}$; D. $5\frac{1}{3}$, $1\frac{1}{2}$, $4\frac{1}{2}$; E. $1\frac{1}{3}$, $2\frac{2}{3}$, $4\frac{1}{4}$; F. $6\frac{1}{3}$, $4\frac{3}{4}$, $7\frac{1}{2}$

Page 62

A. $\frac{9}{12}$, $\frac{12}{15}$, $\frac{4}{6}$; B. $\frac{4}{16}$, $\frac{15}{18}$, $\frac{12}{20}$; C. $\frac{15}{24}$, $\frac{4}{14}$, $\frac{10}{12}$

Page 63

A. $\frac{4}{8}$, $\frac{20}{30}$, $\frac{15}{20}$; B. $\frac{9}{15}$, $\frac{10}{50}$, $\frac{44}{48}$; C. $\frac{3}{12}$, $\frac{36}{81}$, $\frac{10}{18}$; D. $\frac{5}{15}$, $\frac{6}{21}$, $\frac{12}{16}$

Page 64

A. 15, $\frac{10}{15}$, $\frac{12}{15}$; 6, $\frac{3}{6}$, $\frac{2}{6}$; 10, $\frac{4}{10}$, $\frac{5}{10}$

B. 20, $\frac{15}{20}$, $\frac{4}{20}$; 21, $\frac{3}{21}$, $\frac{14}{21}$; 21, $\frac{18}{21}$, $\frac{7}{21}$

C. 10, $\frac{5}{10}$, $\frac{6}{10}$; 14, $\frac{8}{14}$, $\frac{7}{14}$; 24, $\frac{16}{24}$, $\frac{15}{24}$

Page 65

A. 6, $\frac{4}{6} + \frac{5}{6} = \frac{9}{6}$; 4, $\frac{2}{4} - \frac{1}{4} = \frac{1}{4}$; 10, $\frac{4}{10} + \frac{1}{10} = \frac{5}{10}$;

B. 12, $\frac{9}{12} + \frac{1}{12} = \frac{10}{12}$; 14, $\frac{2}{14} - \frac{2}{14} = \frac{0}{14}$; 9, $\frac{6}{9} - \frac{3}{9} = \frac{3}{9}$; C. 10, $\frac{1}{10} + \frac{6}{10} = \frac{7}{10}$; 8, $\frac{3}{8} + \frac{4}{8} = \frac{7}{8}$; 8, $\frac{6}{8} - \frac{5}{8} = \frac{1}{8}$

Page 66

A. 2, B. $\frac{1}{4}$ cup, C. $\frac{5}{2}$ tsp., D. 7 $\frac{1}{2}$ cups of coconut;

E. 2 $\frac{1}{2}$ cups of raisins; F. coconut

Page 67

A. $\frac{3}{8}$, $\frac{3}{4}$, $\frac{1}{2}$, $\frac{1}{6}$; B. 2 $\frac{2}{3}$, 1 $\frac{2}{5}$, 4 $\frac{1}{2}$; C. $\frac{11}{4}$, $\frac{31}{7}$,

$\frac{11}{2}$; D. $\frac{2}{3}$, $\frac{1}{3}$, $\frac{2}{9}$; E. $\frac{12}{16}$, $\frac{14}{21}$, $\frac{3}{18}$; F. 4 slices; G. $\frac{1}{4}$

Page 68

A. 2 $\frac{1}{3}$, 2 $\frac{1}{5}$, 2 $\frac{1}{2}$, 1 $\frac{1}{8}$; B. $\frac{8}{5}$, $\frac{14}{3}$, $\frac{31}{6}$, $\frac{29}{8}$; C. $\frac{3}{4}$,

$\frac{1}{3}$, $\frac{1}{8}$, $\frac{3}{10}$; D. $\frac{3}{12}$, $\frac{16}{24}$, $\frac{20}{25}$, $\frac{6}{27}$; E. $\frac{1}{4}$; F. $\frac{9}{17}$

Page 69

A. $\frac{1}{2}$, $\frac{1}{2}$, $\frac{2}{2}$ or 1; B. $\frac{1}{4}$, $\frac{2}{4}$, $\frac{3}{4}$ (Three-fourths of the

object should be shaded.); C. $\frac{3}{8}$, (Two-eighths of the

object should be shaded.), $\frac{5}{8}$ (Five-eighths of the

object should be shaded.); D. (One-sixth of the objects

should be shaded.), $\frac{4}{6}$, $\frac{5}{6}$, (Five-sixths of the object

should be shaded.)

Page 70

A. $\frac{4}{5}$, $\frac{2}{3}$, $\frac{2}{3}$, $\frac{1}{3}$; B. $\frac{3}{7}$, $\frac{1}{2}$, $\frac{5}{12}$, $\frac{7}{10}$;

C. $\frac{5}{6}$, $\frac{4}{11}$, $\frac{3}{4}$, $\frac{7}{9}$; D. $\frac{4}{9}$, $\frac{2}{3}$, $\frac{7}{11}$, $\frac{7}{8}$

Page 71

A. 1, 1 $\frac{1}{3}$, 1 $\frac{1}{7}$, $\frac{1}{2}$; B. 1 $\frac{1}{5}$, $\frac{1}{2}$, 1, 1 $\frac{1}{2}$;

C. 1 $\frac{2}{7}$, $\frac{5}{8}$, 1 $\frac{2}{3}$, $\frac{2}{3}$; D. 1 $\frac{1}{5}$, 1 $\frac{1}{2}$, 1 $\frac{1}{4}$, 1 $\frac{1}{3}$

Page 72

A. 5 $\frac{2}{3}$, 4 $\frac{3}{5}$, 6, 13 $\frac{1}{2}$; B. 6 $\frac{1}{5}$, 14 $\frac{1}{2}$, 4 $\frac{1}{2}$, 6 $\frac{3}{7}$;

C. 13, 6 $\frac{1}{3}$, 4 $\frac{1}{10}$, 4 $\frac{4}{5}$; D. 5 $\frac{3}{4}$, 8 $\frac{1}{3}$, 18 $\frac{1}{3}$, 41 $\frac{1}{10}$

Page 73

A. $\frac{11}{15}$, $\frac{17}{24}$, $\frac{5}{6}$, 1 $\frac{7}{20}$; B. 1 $\frac{7}{30}$, $\frac{20}{21}$, $\frac{19}{30}$, 1 $\frac{1}{18}$;

C. $\frac{25}{28}$, $\frac{23}{24}$, 1 $\frac{1}{12}$, 1 $\frac{11}{30}$

Page 74

A. 1 $\frac{1}{9}$, $\frac{7}{8}$, $\frac{7}{10}$, 1 $\frac{1}{8}$; B. 1 $\frac{1}{6}$, $\frac{7}{15}$, $\frac{5}{6}$, 1 $\frac{5}{8}$;

C. 1 $\frac{3}{8}$, $\frac{7}{8}$, $\frac{13}{14}$, 1 $\frac{1}{4}$

Page 75

A. 5 $\frac{13}{24}$, 5 $\frac{19}{20}$, 7 $\frac{1}{6}$, 5 $\frac{11}{12}$; B. 8 $\frac{1}{4}$, 7 $\frac{11}{15}$, 6 $\frac{11}{12}$, 4 $\frac{1}{24}$;

C. 7 $\frac{1}{4}$, 5 $\frac{1}{10}$, 9 $\frac{7}{8}$, 12 $\frac{3}{22}$

Page 76

A. $\frac{1}{2}$, $\frac{1}{2}$, $\frac{2}{5}$, 1 $\frac{1}{3}$; B. 2 $\frac{2}{3}$, 9, 3, 9 $\frac{1}{3}$;

C. 3 $\frac{15}{28}$, 5 $\frac{26}{35}$, 6 $\frac{1}{11}$, 1 $\frac{1}{6}$; D. 1 $\frac{11}{24}$, $\frac{19}{20}$, $\frac{3}{5}$, $\frac{13}{24}$;

E. 8 $\frac{1}{6}$, 7 $\frac{11}{24}$, 6 $\frac{5}{18}$, 4 $\frac{1}{2}$

Page 77

A. $\frac{1}{4}$, $\frac{1}{6}$, $\frac{2}{3}$, $\frac{3}{7}$; B. $\frac{5}{6}$, $\frac{3}{5}$, $\frac{2}{3}$, $\frac{1}{3}$; C. $\frac{1}{2}$, $\frac{1}{2}$, $\frac{7}{11}$, $\frac{5}{8}$

Page 78

A. 4 $\frac{1}{8}$, 2 $\frac{2}{3}$, 5 $\frac{2}{9}$, 3 $\frac{3}{5}$; B. 7 $\frac{1}{5}$, 4 $\frac{5}{9}$, 11 $\frac{8}{11}$, 8 $\frac{1}{9}$;

C. 6 $\frac{2}{3}$, 9 $\frac{4}{5}$, 11 $\frac{3}{10}$, 7 $\frac{1}{6}$

ANSWER KEY

Page 79

A. $1\frac{5}{7}$, $2\frac{2}{3}$, $1\frac{1}{3}$, $5\frac{3}{4}$; B. $2\frac{3}{5}$, $\frac{3}{5}$, $2\frac{3}{5}$, $2\frac{5}{6}$;

C. $\frac{1}{2}$, $\frac{2}{3}$, $1\frac{5}{6}$, $5\frac{1}{2}$

Page 80

A. $2\frac{1}{2}$, $1\frac{6}{7}$, $\frac{1}{2}$, $1\frac{3}{4}$; B. $2\frac{1}{2}$, $1\frac{6}{7}$, $2\frac{1}{4}$, $4\frac{3}{5}$;

C. $\frac{2}{7}$, $2\frac{3}{5}$, $3\frac{3}{5}$, $3\frac{1}{3}$; D. $\frac{9}{11}$, $\frac{2}{3}$, $2\frac{4}{5}$, $\frac{1}{2}$;

E. $4\frac{1}{2}$, $5\frac{5}{7}$, $4\frac{1}{2}$, $9\frac{2}{3}$

Page 81

A. $\frac{5}{12}$, $\frac{3}{10}$, $\frac{1}{6}$, $\frac{3}{14}$; B. $\frac{5}{18}$, $\frac{8}{21}$, $\frac{11}{20}$, $\frac{18}{35}$;

C. $\frac{17}{45}$, $\frac{19}{40}$, $\frac{29}{42}$, $\frac{43}{66}$

Page 82

A. $\frac{1}{20}$, $\frac{11}{18}$, $\frac{1}{8}$, $\frac{4}{9}$; B. $\frac{1}{3}$, $\frac{1}{5}$, $\frac{3}{8}$, $\frac{1}{10}$;

C. $\frac{11}{24}$, $\frac{8}{15}$, $\frac{7}{12}$, $\frac{1}{24}$

Page 83

A. $\frac{1}{6}$, $\frac{19}{30}$, $\frac{7}{12}$, $\frac{1}{10}$; B. $\frac{3}{8}$, $\frac{1}{5}$, $\frac{1}{4}$, $\frac{3}{8}$;

C. $\frac{7}{24}$, $\frac{1}{2}$, $\frac{4}{9}$, $\frac{7}{18}$; D. $\frac{11}{24}$, $\frac{1}{6}$, $\frac{5}{12}$, $\frac{1}{3}$;

E. $\frac{1}{2}$, $\frac{7}{20}$, $\frac{1}{12}$, $\frac{2}{15}$

Page 84

A. $1\frac{5}{6}$, $\frac{23}{24}$, $1\frac{3}{4}$, $3\frac{4}{15}$; B. $\frac{5}{8}$, $\frac{5}{9}$, $1\frac{5}{6}$, $1\frac{7}{10}$;

C. $1\frac{17}{24}$, $3\frac{3}{8}$, $3\frac{1}{2}$, $\frac{3}{4}$

Page 85

A. $\frac{1}{2}$, $\frac{4}{21}$, $2\frac{2}{3}$, $5\frac{1}{8}$; B. $\frac{3}{10}$, $\frac{1}{8}$, $2\frac{1}{2}$, $7\frac{1}{2}$;

C. $\frac{1}{3}$, $6\frac{1}{2}$, $6\frac{5}{12}$, $1\frac{8}{15}$; D. $9\frac{2}{5}$, 4 , $\frac{10}{33}$, $\frac{7}{24}$;

E. 9 , $\frac{1}{6}$, $1\frac{1}{6}$, $\frac{5}{8}$

Page 86

A. $\frac{5}{12}$; B. $\frac{11}{12}$, $\frac{1}{12}$; C. $\frac{3}{4}$, $\frac{1}{4}$; D. $6\frac{1}{4}$ minutes

Page 87

A. $3\frac{11}{12}$ hours; B. $\frac{7}{12}$ hour; C. $\frac{2}{3}$ hour; D. $2\frac{5}{12}$ hours;

E. $1\frac{1}{12}$ hours; F. Tyrell

Page 88

A. $\frac{4}{5}$, $\frac{1}{2}$, $1\frac{3}{5}$, 1 ; B. $3\frac{1}{2}$, $5\frac{2}{3}$, $16\frac{2}{7}$, 13 ;

C. $\frac{3}{4}$, $1\frac{3}{5}$, $\frac{1}{2}$, $1\frac{5}{6}$; D. $\frac{1}{12}$, $\frac{11}{24}$, $5\frac{2}{7}$, $4\frac{13}{15}$;

D. $\frac{2}{9}$; F. $\frac{13}{16}$

Page 89

A. $\frac{4}{7}$, 1 , $\frac{2}{3}$, $1\frac{2}{3}$; B. $3\frac{2}{5}$, 9 , 11 , $4\frac{1}{2}$;

C. $\frac{1}{2}$, $3\frac{2}{5}$, $1\frac{1}{2}$, $3\frac{2}{3}$; D. $\frac{1}{2}$, $\frac{1}{12}$, $6\frac{4}{7}$, $12\frac{1}{3}$;

E. yes; F. $\frac{1}{2}$

Page 90

A. $\frac{2}{15}$; B. $\frac{1}{12}$; C. $\frac{1}{4}$; D. $\frac{3}{8}$

MATH SUCCESS RB-904107 © Rainbow Bridge Publishing

ANSWER KEY

Page 91

A. $\frac{3}{8}$, $\frac{2}{15}$, $\frac{2}{15}$, $\frac{5}{12}$; B. $\frac{3}{32}$, $\frac{5}{24}$, $\frac{5}{14}$, $\frac{1}{12}$;

C. $\frac{2}{25}$, $\frac{3}{10}$, $\frac{9}{20}$, $\frac{3}{32}$; D. $\frac{6}{25}$, $\frac{1}{4}$, $\frac{4}{9}$, $\frac{3}{16}$;

E. $\frac{5}{21}$, $\frac{3}{14}$, $\frac{5}{24}$, $\frac{5}{18}$; F. $\frac{3}{35}$, $\frac{1}{16}$, $\frac{3}{28}$, $\frac{5}{18}$

Page 92

A. $\frac{1}{4}$, $\frac{2}{5}$, $\frac{2}{7}$, $\frac{2}{7}$; B. $\frac{5}{9}$, $\frac{1}{10}$, $\frac{1}{3}$, $\frac{1}{4}$;

C. $\frac{1}{16}$, $\frac{4}{7}$, $\frac{1}{12}$, $\frac{2}{6}$; D. $\frac{3}{16}$, $\frac{2}{15}$, $\frac{2}{7}$, $\frac{1}{6}$

Page 93

A. 2, $1\frac{3}{5}$, $\frac{6}{7}$, $1\frac{1}{7}$; B. $2\frac{2}{5}$, $\frac{9}{10}$, $6\frac{3}{4}$, $1\frac{4}{5}$;

C. $1\frac{1}{3}$, $1\frac{5}{7}$, $\frac{3}{5}$, $1\frac{1}{2}$; D. $1\frac{1}{2}$, $1\frac{1}{9}$, $\frac{6}{7}$, $2\frac{2}{3}$

Page 94

A. $\frac{9}{16}$, $2\frac{1}{3}$, $1\frac{1}{2}$, $1\frac{1}{7}$; B. $\frac{7}{8}$, $2\frac{1}{10}$, $1\frac{1}{3}$, $3\frac{1}{2}$;

C. $1\frac{7}{12}$, $\frac{5}{18}$, $\frac{4}{5}$, $\frac{5}{9}$; D. $3\frac{1}{2}$, $1\frac{7}{12}$, $1\frac{9}{16}$, $\frac{7}{8}$

Page 95

A. $6\frac{1}{2}$, $3\frac{3}{5}$, $3\frac{6}{7}$, $9\frac{1}{7}$; B. $6\frac{4}{5}$, $6\frac{9}{10}$, $15\frac{3}{4}$, $12\frac{9}{10}$; C. $12\frac{1}{2}$, $7\frac{5}{7}$, $12\frac{3}{5}$, $21\frac{1}{2}$; D. $9\frac{1}{5}$, $12\frac{7}{9}$, $10\frac{2}{7}$, $26\frac{2}{3}$

Page 96

A. 10, $3\frac{1}{8}$, $4\frac{19}{20}$, $2\frac{3}{5}$; B. $2\frac{6}{25}$, $8\frac{1}{3}$, $7\frac{1}{2}$, $14\frac{7}{10}$;

C. $5\frac{13}{24}$, $2\frac{1}{4}$, $1\frac{27}{28}$, $5\frac{1}{2}$; D. $6\frac{3}{10}$, 4, $6\frac{3}{4}$, $7\frac{45}{56}$

Page 97

A. $\frac{3}{8}$, $\frac{2}{15}$, $\frac{4}{15}$, $\frac{15}{32}$; B. $\frac{2}{5}$, $\frac{4}{9}$, $\frac{3}{10}$, $\frac{2}{11}$; C. 2, $2\frac{1}{2}$, $5\frac{1}{3}$, $5\frac{3}{5}$; D. 1, $\frac{3}{5}$, $\frac{3}{4}$, $1\frac{7}{8}$; E. $13\frac{3}{4}$, 3, 11, $5\frac{1}{3}$

Page 98

A. $2\frac{2}{5}$ miles; B. $\frac{3}{5}$ gallon; C. $4.00; D. $\frac{1}{4}$; E. $\frac{3}{5}$ mile;

F. $60\frac{2}{3}$ hours

Page 99

A. 3 students; B. 9 girls; C. 4 students; D. $\frac{3}{4}$ hour;

E. $1\frac{1}{6}$ hours; F. 4 students

Page 100

A. $\frac{4}{15}$, $\frac{8}{33}$, $\frac{3}{11}$, $\frac{10}{21}$; B. $5\frac{1}{4}$, $1\frac{4}{5}$, $1\frac{1}{5}$, $1\frac{11}{24}$;

C. 7, $7\frac{1}{2}$, 10, $1\frac{2}{3}$; D. $4\frac{3}{8}$, 4, $8\frac{2}{5}$, $7\frac{11}{30}$;

E. $6\frac{2}{3}$ hours, $8\frac{1}{4}$ cups of oats

Page 101

A. $\frac{5}{24}$, $\frac{7}{30}$, $\frac{1}{14}$, $\frac{3}{8}$; B. 6, $1\frac{2}{3}$, $1\frac{5}{7}$, $2\frac{1}{12}$; C. $1\frac{7}{8}$, $3\frac{2}{3}$, $6\frac{1}{4}$, $16\frac{1}{2}$; D. $6\frac{8}{9}$, $6\frac{5}{12}$, 2, $5\frac{2}{3}$; E. 12 hours; F. 3 miles

Page 102

A. $\frac{3}{10}$; B. one and twelve hundredths, $1\frac{12}{100}$; C. 0.221;

$\frac{221}{1000}$; D. 0.53, fifty-three hundredths; E. eight hundred

seventy-one thousandths, $\frac{871}{1000}$; F. 0.05, five hundredths;

G. seven hundred eighty-three thousandths, $\frac{783}{1000}$;

H. 2.6, $2\frac{6}{10}$; I. 0.115, one hundred fifteen thousandths

ANSWER KEY

Page 103

A. 5.78, 0.23; B. 1.03, 0.5; C. 0.548, 2.53; D. 53.17, 16.303

E. 0.091, 91.3; F. $2\frac{87}{100}$, $\frac{983}{1000}$; G. $14\frac{5}{10}$, $287\frac{69}{100}$;

H. $1\frac{752}{1000}$, $\frac{7}{10}$; I. $\frac{6}{100}$, $10\frac{54}{1000}$; J. $81\frac{2}{10}$, $\frac{157}{1000}$

Page 104

A. $\frac{2}{10}$, 0.2; B. $\frac{8}{10}$, 0.8; C. $\frac{9}{10}$, 0.9; D. $\frac{1}{10}$, 0.1;

E. $\frac{13}{100}$, 0.13; F. $\frac{87}{100}$, 0.87; G. $\frac{55}{100}$, 0.55

Page 105

A. < , < , < ; B. > , > , >; C. > , > , < ; D. < , < , = ;
E. < , > , = ; F. < , < , >

Page 106

A. $1.05, $1.07, $1.10, $1.25, $2.03, $2.15, $2.21, $2.51;
B. 4.55; C. 10.75; D. 2.52; E. 1.847; F. 89.90

Page 107

A. 3 ft.; B. 8 in.; C. 5 yd.; D. 5; 60; E. 14; 10,560; F. 87;
16,150; G. 158; 69; H. 5,530 feet; I. 4 inches

Page 108

A. 11 m; B. m; C. cm; D. 420; 4,000; 850;
E. 500 centimeters; F. 35 kilometers

Page 109

A. 2 cups; B. 60 gal.; C. 2 gal.; D. 2 qt.; E. 10, 2; F. 4, 2;
G. 12, 4; H. 88, 9; I. 9, 4; J. 11, 24; K. 11, 135; L. 29, 10

Page 110

A. 3.8 L; B. 5 mL; C. 1 kL; D. 1 mL; E. 2,000, 5,000, 24,000;
F. 2, 45, 38,000; G. 5 kg; H. 5 mL; I. 7,000, 6, 73;
J. 4,000 grams

Page 111

A. 14, 16; B. 12, 9; C. 12, 11.6

Page 112

A. 12; B. 24; C. 14; D. 12; E. 35; F. 30

Page 113

A. 12; B. 25; C. 20; D. 84; E. 18; F. 4; G. 30; H. 15; I. 5

Page 114

A. line; B. ray; C. line segment; D. intersecting; E. parallel;
F. intersecting; G. perpendicular

Page 115

A. acute, right; B. right, obtuse; C. obtuse, acute;
D. obtuse, acute; E. right, acute

Page 116

A. pentagon; B. quadrilateral; C. triangle; D. heptagon;
E. pentagon; F. octagon

Page 117

A. congruent, similar; B. congruent, similar;
C. similar, similar

Page 118

A. cylinder, rectangular prism; B. triangular prism, cone;
C. pyramid, sphere

Page 119

A. 6, 12; B. 5, 9; C. 6, 12; D. 8, 18

Page 120

A.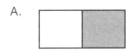
B.
C.
D.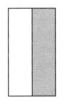

MATH SUCCESS RB-904107

$\frac{1}{100}$	$\frac{2}{100}$	$\frac{3}{100}$	$\frac{4}{100}$
0.5	0.3$\overline{3}$	0.25	0.2
© RB-904107	© RB-904107	© RB-904107	© RB-904107

$\frac{5}{100}$	$\frac{6}{100}$	$\frac{7}{100}$	$\frac{8}{100}$
0.1$\overline{6}$	0.125	0.1$\overline{1}$	0.1
© RB-904107	© RB-904107	© RB-904107	© RB-904107

$\frac{9}{100}$	$\frac{10}{100}$	$\frac{15}{100}$	$\frac{20}{100}$
0.6$\overline{6}$	0.75	0.4	0.6
© RB-904107	© RB-904107	© RB-904107	© RB-904107

$\frac{25}{100}$	$\frac{30}{100}$	$\frac{35}{100}$	$\frac{40}{100}$
0.8	0.8$\overline{3}$	0.625	0.875
© RB-904107	© RB-904107	© RB-904107	© RB-904107

$\dfrac{1}{5}$ 0.04 © RB-904107	$\dfrac{1}{4}$ 0.03 © RB-904107	$\dfrac{1}{3}$ 0.02 © RB-904107	$\dfrac{1}{2}$ 0.01 © RB-904107
$\dfrac{1}{10}$ 0.08 © RB-904107	$\dfrac{1}{9}$ 0.07 © RB-904107	$\dfrac{1}{8}$ 0.06 © RB-904107	$\dfrac{1}{6}$ 0.05 © RB-904107
$\dfrac{3}{5}$ 0.2 © RB-904107	$\dfrac{2}{5}$ 0.15 © RB-904107	$\dfrac{3}{4}$ 0.1 © RB-904107	$\dfrac{2}{3}$ 0.09 © RB-904107
$\dfrac{7}{8}$ 0.4 © RB-904107	$\dfrac{5}{8}$ 0.35 © RB-904107	$\dfrac{5}{6}$ 0.3 © RB-904107	$\dfrac{4}{5}$ 0.25 © RB-904107

15% $\dfrac{1}{2}$ © RB-904107	**35%** $\dfrac{1}{3}$ © RB-904107	**45%** $\dfrac{1}{4}$ © RB-904107	**55%** $\dfrac{1}{5}$ © RB-904107
65% $\dfrac{1}{6}$ © RB-904107	**70%** $\dfrac{1}{8}$ © RB-904107	**5%** $\dfrac{1}{10}$ © RB-904107	**12%** $\dfrac{2}{3}$ © RB-904107
7% $\dfrac{3}{4}$ © RB-904107	**16%** $\dfrac{2}{5}$ © RB-904107	**18%** $\dfrac{3}{5}$ © RB-904107	**22%** $\dfrac{4}{5}$ © RB-904107
24% $\dfrac{5}{6}$ © RB-904107	**26%** $\dfrac{5}{8}$ © RB-904107	**28%** $\dfrac{7}{8}$ © RB-904107	**30%** $\dfrac{9}{10}$ © RB-904107

20%	25%	33.$\overline{3}$%	50%
$\dfrac{11}{20}$	$\dfrac{9}{20}$	$\dfrac{7}{20}$	$\dfrac{3}{20}$

66.$\overline{6}$%	10%	12.5%	16.$\overline{6}$%
$\dfrac{3}{25}$	$\dfrac{1}{20}$	$\dfrac{7}{10}$	$\dfrac{13}{20}$

80%	60%	40%	75%
$\dfrac{11}{50}$	$\dfrac{9}{50}$	$\dfrac{4}{25}$	$\dfrac{7}{100}$

90%	87.5%	62.5%	83.$\overline{3}$%
$\dfrac{3}{10}$	$\dfrac{7}{25}$	$\dfrac{13}{50}$	$\dfrac{6}{25}$

13% 0.1 © RB-904107	100% 0.15 © RB-904107	95% 0.2 © RB-904107	90% 0.25 © RB-904107
62% 0.3 © RB-904107	58% 0.35 © RB-904107	34% 0.4 © RB-904107	27% 0.45 © RB-904107
22% 0.5 © RB-904107	96% 0.55 © RB-904107	81% 0.6 © RB-904107	79% 0.65 © RB-904107
88% 0.7 © RB-904107	72% 0.75 © RB-904107	57% 0.8 © RB-904107	46% 0.85 © RB-904107

25%	**20%**	**15%**	**10%**
0.9	0.95	1.0	0.13
© RB-904107	© RB-904107	© RB-904107	© RB-904107

45%	**40%**	**35%**	**30%**
0.27	0.34	0.58	0.62
© RB-904107	© RB-904107	© RB-904107	© RB-904107

65%	**60%**	**55%**	**50%**
0.79	0.81	0.96	0.22
© RB-904107	© RB-904107	© RB-904107	© RB-904107

85%	**80%**	**75%**	**70%**
0.46	0.57	0.72	0.88
© RB-904107	© RB-904107	© RB-904107	© RB-904107

0.04 $\dfrac{1}{2}$ © RB-904107	0.03 $\dfrac{1}{3}$ © RB-904107	0.02 $\dfrac{1}{4}$ © RB-904107	0.01 $\dfrac{1}{5}$ © RB-904107
0.08 $\dfrac{1}{6}$ © RB-904107	0.07 $\dfrac{1}{8}$ © RB-904107	0.06 $\dfrac{1}{10}$ © RB-904107	0.05 $\dfrac{2}{3}$ © RB-904107
0.2 $\dfrac{3}{4}$ © RB-904107	0.15 $\dfrac{2}{5}$ © RB-904107	0.1 $\dfrac{3}{5}$ © RB-904107	0.09 $\dfrac{4}{5}$ © RB-904107
0.4 $\dfrac{5}{6}$ © RB-904107	0.35 $\dfrac{5}{8}$ © RB-904107	0.3 $\dfrac{7}{8}$ © RB-904107	0.25 $\dfrac{9}{10}$ © RB-904107

0.2 $$\frac{1}{100}$$ © RB-904107	**0.25** $$\frac{2}{100}$$ © RB-904107	**0.3$\overline{3}$** $$\frac{3}{100}$$ © RB-904107	**0.5** $$\frac{4}{100}$$ © RB-904107
0.6$\overline{6}$ $$\frac{5}{100}$$ © RB-904107	**0.1** $$\frac{6}{100}$$ © RB-904107	**0.125** $$\frac{7}{100}$$ © RB-904107	**0.1$\overline{6}$** $$\frac{8}{100}$$ © RB-904107
0.8 $$\frac{9}{100}$$ © RB-904107	**0.6** $$\frac{10}{100}$$ © RB-904107	**0.4** $$\frac{15}{100}$$ © RB-904107	**0.75** $$\frac{20}{100}$$ © RB-904107
0.9 $$\frac{25}{100}$$ © RB-904107	**0.875** $$\frac{30}{100}$$ © RB-904107	**0.625** $$\frac{35}{100}$$ © RB-904107	**0.8$\overline{3}$** $$\frac{40}{100}$$ © RB-904107

$\frac{3}{20}$	$\frac{7}{20}$	$\frac{9}{20}$	$\frac{11}{20}$
50%	33.$\overline{3}$%	25%	20%

$\frac{13}{20}$	$\frac{7}{10}$	$\frac{4}{5}$	$\frac{3}{25}$
16.$\overline{6}$%	12.5%	10%	66.$\overline{6}$%

$\frac{7}{50}$	$\frac{4}{25}$	$\frac{9}{50}$	$\frac{11}{50}$
75%	40%	60%	80%

$\frac{6}{25}$	$\frac{13}{50}$	$\frac{7}{25}$	$\frac{3}{10}$
83.$\overline{3}$%	62.5%	87.5%	90%

$\frac{1}{5}$	$\frac{1}{4}$	$\frac{1}{3}$	$\frac{1}{2}$
55%	**45%**	**35%**	**15%**
© RB-904107	© RB-904107	© RB-904107	© RB-904107

$\frac{2}{3}$	$\frac{1}{10}$	$\frac{1}{8}$	$\frac{1}{6}$
12%	**80%**	**70%**	**65%**
© RB-904107	© RB-904107	© RB-904107	© RB-904107

$\frac{4}{5}$	$\frac{3}{5}$	$\frac{2}{5}$	$\frac{3}{4}$
22%	**18%**	**16%**	**14%**
© RB-904107	© RB-904107	© RB-904107	© RB-904107

$\frac{9}{10}$	$\frac{7}{8}$	$\frac{5}{8}$	$\frac{5}{6}$
30%	**28%**	**26%**	**24%**
© RB-904107	© RB-904107	© RB-904107	© RB-904107

0.13	1.0	0.95	0.9
25%	20%	15%	10%
© RB-904107	© RB-904107	© RB-904107	© RB-904107

0.62	0.58	0.34	0.27
45%	40%	35%	30%
© RB-904107	© RB-904107	© RB-904107	© RB-904107

0.22	0.96	0.81	0.79
65%	60%	55%	50%
© RB-904107	© RB-904107	© RB-904107	© RB-904107

0.88	0.72	0.57	0.46
85%	80%	75%	70%
© RB-904107	© RB-904107	© RB-904107	© RB-904107

0.1	0.15	0.2	0.25
90%	95%	100%	13%
© RB-904107	© RB-904107	© RB-904107	© RB-904107

0.3	0.35	0.4	0.45
27%	34%	58%	62%
© RB-904107	© RB-904107	© RB-904107	© RB-904107

0.5	0.55	0.6	0.65
79%	81%	96%	22%
© RB-904107	© RB-904107	© RB-904107	© RB-904107

0.7	0.75	0.8	0.85
46%	57%	72%	88%
© RB-904107	© RB-904107	© RB-904107	© RB-904107